The Potter's Touch

God Calls Us to Life

by

William Reiser, S. J.

Paulist Press   *New York/Ramsey*

Library of Congress
Catalog Card Number: 81-82339

ISBN: 0-8091-2404-1

Published by Paulist Press
545 Island Road, Ramsey, N. J. 07446

Printed and bound in the
United States of America

Contents

Introduction

This is a short book about creation. It is not so much about how God put the universe together as about how he put us together, endowing us with spirit and mind in order that we should become fully people of God. The process of creation continues to unfold in us, and as that process goes along we experience our creaturehood. In the course of those experiences we manage to glimpse what God has been doing throughout the ages as he fashions a people after his own heart.

In the summer of 1977, I was invited to give a series of talks on spirituality to St. Mary's Parish in Oak Ridge, Tennessee. Since the precise nature of the talks had not been specified, I selected more or less at random five topics in the history of spirituality. The talks centered around documents like the *Didache* (dating from the late first or early second century), St. Athanasius' *Life of Antony* from the fourth century, the anonymously written work *The Cloud of Unknowing* (a beautiful mystical writing dating from fourteenth-century England), Teilhard de Chardin's *Hymn of the Universe,* an essay by Thomas Merton on solitude, and some of Gandhi's thoughts on non-violence.

What emerged throughout the week, however, was a kind of spiritual architecture in which the central piece was the prayer of desire in Christian life. That actively desiring God should be important for spiritual growth came as no surprise. But the consistency of that theme throughout different centuries and spiritual traditions seemed remarkable. The desire for God is something which we experience, something which believers recognize in themselves as nothing less than their desire for life. It plays the significant part in our ongoing creation as people of God. Letting that desire unfold is what initiates, nourishes, sustains, and carries forward the life of God within us. Noticing how that desire moves becomes the key to spiritual discernment. Allowing that desire to take over our mind and heart opens up the path to purification of soul and union with God. Discovering that God himself is the source and term of that desire brings joy. The desire unfolds dynamically through charity, for in desiring God above all things we grow to be like the very thing which we desire. We are transformed by what we love.

Several times since August 1977 I have offered the same series of lectures and included other readings such as *The Confessions of Saint Augustine* and St. Bonaventure's *The Soul's Journey into God.* But each time my own appreciation of the prayer of desire was enhanced because of the questions and the freely shared experiences of those who came to listen. One evening, for example, when we were discussing *The Cloud of Unknowing,* a gentleman asked whether such spiritual heights were attainable in our own day. Someone answered that if familiarity with God and deep, silent love were the marks of a mystic, then she knew quite a few mystics in her own parish. It was a good reminder that experiencing God should hardly be unusual for men and women who are trying to live out the Gospel, but it is important to help people to notice how God is moving in their experience. To identify his action is essential if we are to taste the peace of his presence. People who are feeling a desire for life—which is after all a desire for God who is life—are usually gladdened by the assurance that the desire itself is from God. As they begin to notice the dimensions of that desire in their lives, their sense of God's presence is enriched. I have found this to be true in my own experience, and my belief has been confirmed by the experiences of those people who have shared some of their life with me. It is no wonder, then, that there has been such a lively resurgence of interest in contemplative prayer and spiritual direction in the last few years.

Let me offer a brief explanation on the arrangement of the chapters. The first one is intended to heighten the reader's awareness of God's investment in the work of creation and to suggest that in creating the world God has, as it were, put his reputation on the line. Although the context of the passage was quite different, the words of Luke 14:28–30 could apply to God's decision to get involved with the human race:

> Suppose one of you wants to build a tower. Will he not first sit down and estimate the cost to see if he has enough money to complete it? For if he lays the foundations and is not able to finish it, everyone who sees it will ridicule him, saying, "This fellow began to build and was not able to finish."

This line of thinking raises further questions about how we are to think of God. Chapter 2 treats at some length what being people of God means, and Chapter 3 draws the conclusion that only people who are of God can recognize what is true. People have been talking about orthodoxy and heresy lately, but it seems to me that a Christian cannot adequately talk about truth apart from its relationship to prayer and the spiritual life. The language of those chapters may sound occasionally academic, but the concern is quite down-to-earth. Religious people must be concerned about truth because the truths of faith are intended to draw the human spirit to life, and those truths are confirmed as life-giving through the spiritual experience of the Christian tradition. The ideas there are important and need to be understood if the Christian message itself is not to be trivialized into a religion of moral precepts and external observance. Otherwise Christianity can become a religion with doctrines which have not been sufficiently related to the life of faith.

The fourth chapter is concerned with our becoming free enough to accept God on his own terms, and we learn a great deal about the nature of freedom by contemplating the freedom of God. There cannot be genuine spiritual life apart from freedom, while the struggle to realize our freedom takes many directions. Yet our freedom is not won through preoccupation with our personal self-fulfillment. It is achieved as we allow ourselves to be shaped according to the image of Christ. The redemption of human freedom takes place as we turn regularly and lovingly toward the God who has showed himself to us in Christ. This demands leaving God room to show himself as he truly is and not as we presume he ought to behave. Such is the theme behind Chapter 5.

The final chapter is brief and serves as an epilogue. It continues the theme of creation by reflecting on the respect that creatures should show toward the workmanship of God. We are, after all, a people who live in God's neighborhood, since he has taken up his dwelling among us (Jn. 1:14). He is always near to those who would like to call upon him (Ps. 145:18). I have drawn somewhat on an insight from the philosopher Martin Heidegger which appears in a book of collected essays entitled *The Piety of Thinking*. Because God and the human family are in some sense neighbors on the earth, our manners should be appropriate. We are asked to be reverent. If our manners may be described in terms of reverence, God's manner toward us is described by compassion. Who is my neighbor? The one who shows me mercy (Lk. 10:36–37).

Throughout the book I have used the New International Version of the Bible for the scriptural texts. These pages grew with my preaching and teaching, and so I am glad for the opportunity to acknowledge my gratitude to the people of the Cathedral of the Incarnation parish in Nashville, Tennessee. For five years, from 1973 to 1978, they listened to my sermons, encouraging me by their attentiveness and supporting me with their prayers. I am also thankful for my students at Holy Cross who have joined me in reflecting upon the idea and experience of Christian faith. And I owe so much to the spiritual insight of close friends in the Society of Jesus, my companions in faith. But it is to my family, to my father and mother, that this book really belongs, for they introduced me to the way of Christ.

Holy Cross College
Worcester, Massachusetts

1 God Has an
Investment in Creation

Two books of the Bible open with the same phrase. "In the beginning," wrote the author of the Book of Genesis, "God created the heavens and the earth." And he continued:

> Now the surface was formless and empty, darkness was over the surface of the deep, and the Spirit of God was hovering over the waters. And God said, "Let there be light," and there was light (Gen. 1:1–3).

Centuries later the evangelist of the Fourth Gospel introduced his work by declaring, "In the beginning was the Word, and the Word was with God, and the Word was God." And he continued:

> Through him all things were made; without him nothing was made that has been made. In him was life, and that life was the light of men. The light shines in the darkness, but the darkness has not understood it (Jn. 1:1–5).

Taken together, these verses confess the basic beauty, simplicity, and harmony of Christian faith. Creation, revelation, and incarnation are the essential pieces of the Christian worldview.

They comprise the foundation of all that we believe about God, and they structure our religious outlook upon the world and human history. If we should wonder why God joined our history through the incarnation of his Son, we would find ourselves pushed to a second question: Why does God want to reveal himself in the first place? Yet this question invites still another, perhaps the most important question of all: Why did God decide to create the world?

These two scriptural passages reflect major religious ideas which have steered the people of God along their journey through history. The heavens and the earth, we believe, come from God—not from chance, not from necessity, not from some evil power, but from God. We also believe that our God is not a God of silence but one who has a word, that is, ours is a God whose very nature it is to speak. God's speech, furthermore, is creative. When he opens his mouth, light bursts into the darkness, suns start to burn and radiate their brilliance, galaxies spin and planets wind into their orbits. When God's all-powerful Word becomes visible, it assumes the form and features of the life and teaching of Jesus of Nazareth. And in Jesus, the Word of God made flesh, men and women discover what human life is supposed to be.

These ideas add up to the simple Christian confession that God decided to create the world in order to communicate life. But God is life, and so it must be said that God created the world in order to share himself. In order to understand what coming to life means, and to understand what it means for God to share himself, Christian faith looks carefully and contemplatively at Jesus Christ. In Jesus, God is present. For those who can hear the God who speaks in Jesus, the word which God speaks is creative: it encounters, renews, transforms, and makes holy. In the Spirit of Jesus, God hovers even now over the formlessness of human lives, just as the Spirit once hovered over the primeval waters of chaos (Gen. 1:2). And as the creative Spirit brought form and light to that empty darkness, so the same Spirit in Christ forms and clarifies our own emptiness, charging our souls with life.·

What Does God Want?

In order to appreciate God's designs for the world, it is worth trying to hear what the universe tells us about itself. The eye of the psalmist was never blind to any information the world could disclose about the Creator; our seeing should be just as keen. In a feature essay of its March 12, 1979 issue commemorating the centennial of Albert Einstein's birth, *Newsweek* magazine assembled the following account:

> In the beginning, there was a big bang. A fireball of pure energy exploded, cooling as it spread outward; in one-hundredth of a second after creation, the temperature of the universe was 100 billion degrees Celsius and its density almost 4 billion times that of water. Particles emerged, turning into energy and back into matter. After three minutes, 46 seconds, the particles held together long enough to create hydrogen and helium nuclei. A half hour later, one-quarter of the hydrogen had changed into helium, determining forever the chemical constitution of the cosmos.
>
> Creation then slowed down. It took 700,000 years, during which the ever-enlarging universe cooled to about 4,000 degrees, for matter to displace radiation as the primary component of the cosmos. The nuclei and electrons combined to form stable hydrogen and helium gas. Soon the clouds of gas coalesced into stars and galaxies. Today, 15 billion to 20 billion years later, the successors of those primordial objects—100 billion galaxies, each containing about 100 billion stars—blanket the night sky, still rushing away from each other as the universe continues to expand.

One particularly striking element of this "record" of the universe's coming-to-be is the enormous stretches of time involved in the production of "this good earth." It would be presumptuous to suggest that our planet was the only target of God's creative plans. Nevertheless, the sheer expense of time and energy called for in order to produce a firmament hospitable to human life should dazzle our imaginations. If we consider all the energies, elements, and opportunities which had to conspire in order to bring about the very possibility of human life, our wonder might be voiced in the humble and astonished cry of the psalmist: "What is man that you are mindful of him, the son of man that you care for him?" (Ps. 8:4).

But notice what happens if the emphasis is shifted from the son of man about whom God is mindful to the "you" who has been addressed: "What is man that *you are mindful* of him, the son of man that *you care for* him?" It is astonishing that God should be interested in us at all, and it is further astonishing that God should want to share his own life (is there any other kind of life?) with his creatures. But faith leads us to marvel even more that if God has been actively concerned to produce a world which would freely accept his life, how much must God want creation to succeed! If it should happen through some terrible misfortune of human anger and greed that the planet earth were erased of life in a nuclear war, then the dreadful waste of possibilities would be measured not only in terms of our individual lives, nor only in terms of the history of human beings on the earth, but in terms of the fifteen to twenty billion years of patient waiting that finally gave birth to life endowed with intelligence and heart. And however tragic and incomprehensible, however bitter and unconsolable our destruction would be for us as we watched the end of our history, could our feelings ever match the disappointment and sadness of the God who is mindful of us, and who cares?

The Divine Investment

To speak about God's investment in the work of his hands should make perfect sense for the Christian. This sense is justified by the incarnation. Christian faith professes its belief in a God who desires to come close to his creatures, to share in their history, to transform their hopes, and to underline once and for all how extremely important we are to him. God's becoming human states clearly and unambiguously the intrinsic worth of human life and history. God wants to be among his creatures; it is as simple as that. After his work of creating the world, God—like the wisdom spoken of in the Book of Proverbs—could be found rejoicing in his whole world and delighting in mankind (Prov. 8:30–31). Is it surprising that eventually the Word should become flesh and live for a while among us (Jn. 1:14)?

For what purpose, then, does God create? Why does he reveal himself? Why would he join our history? Why does he choose to redeem? Christian contemplation answers these questions by saying that God has loved us, and neither theology nor philosophy can add much more. The brevity and simplicity of the answer may be intellectually annoying or even scandalous if we are in a mood for brooding over imponderables. But simple truth turns out to be profound mystery. We are alive, we exist on the earth for no other reason than this, that we have been loved; God has invested his love in us, and the heavens and the earth bear witness to this fact. To press for some further, practical, sensible explanation would only result in frustration. There is no reason to deprive God of the truest, simplest explanation of all, namely, that he is good.

Many parents have waited years for their children to acknowledge the gift of being loved. There are many times, naturally, when mothers and fathers find their patience exhausted by children who seem to take them for granted and rarely give a thought to their parents' feelings. Yet somehow parents retain faith in their children, because they believe that so much care and love spent on them must one day bear fruit. Parents live in hope for the day when a child will realize what love it has received. I remember a father confiding that he would give anything he had in order to have his son come home one day and throw his arms, not around the father (that would have been too much to hope for), but around his mother, and tell her "I love you." The experience of being appreciated, and the desire that those whom we love should also feel appreciated, belong among the truest, simplest, and most welcome experiences that we can enjoy. I can also recall a woman, tearful and broken because someone she loved no longer had any use for her, expressing the bitterest hurt: "If only he knew me, if only he could see how deep in my heart I have loved him, he would never have acted that way toward me!" It is not far-fetched to imagine God saying the same thing.

When Christians kneel before the Lord on the cross, and as they imagine themselves placed alongside Jesus as he suffered for us, it would be out of place to begin a theological speculation about the meaning of redemption. The occasion calls for a prayerful response to God's love. If we start to dialogue with Christ by saying, "You did this to teach us the meaning of love," or "You did this to open for us the gates of heaven," then perhaps we have not yet penetrated enough the mystery of God's love. It would be like a child telling his mother or father at some time, "You have done all these things for me in order to teach me what being a parent is like." Indeed, parents do teach their children about being parents, but how many parents actually think about their vocation in such terms? Most fathers and mothers do not reflect as they feed, clothe, teach, discipline, and watch over their children that they are doing these things simply for the sake of instructing their sons and daughters about rearing children. In the same way, the meeting of a Christian with the crucified Jesus must go beyond the easy explanation of his wanting to teach us (which he does) or of his wanting to leave us an example (which he did). God has invested his love in us, and whatever he does in our regard issues from his own goodness. So much has God loved us that not only does he want to join our history, but he wants to be where his people are, in whatever conditions they must live. And if this desire eventually draws God to face the possibility of death at the hands of those who misunderstand his intentions, then so be it. God will not seek a means of escape. Such love needs to be encountered in the quiet moments of Christian prayer.

The cross sheds a great deal of light on the intensity of God's desire to create the world. It illumines from within how strongly God wants human beings to be in communion with him. God redeems and reveals for the same reason that he creates. Redemption does not happen as an afterthought, or as an attempt to straighten out a creation that went off track because of sin. There is a fundamental continuity which pervades whatever God does. It is his intention that in the universe there should be creatures who can joyfully and gratefully experience and acknowledge how greatly they have been loved. This is to understand the words of the prophet Hosea when he spoke for the Lord:

> When Israel was a child, I loved him, and out of Egypt I called my son. But the more I called Israel, the further they went from me. They sacrificed to the Baals and they burned incense to images.
>
> It was I who taught Ephraim to talk, taking them by the arms; but they did not realize that it was I who healed them.
>
> I led them with cords of human kindness, and ties of love;
>
> I lifted the yoke from their neck and bent down to feed them (Hos. 11:1–4).

God's love for the world is so characteristic of his dealings with the human race that St. Anselm felt free to explain our redemption to the monk, Boso, as something which is appropriate to the nature of God. Anything less than the gift of his Son would have been unbecoming, considering the nature of divine love. Thus Anselm wrote:

> *Anselm:* From all this it is easy to draw a conclusion. Either God will bring to completion what He began in regard to human nature, or it was pointless for Him to create such a sublime nature for so great a good. But if God, so far as we know, has created nothing more precious than a rational nature to find enjoyment in Himself, it would be extremely adverse to Him to allow rational nature to perish completely.

Boso: A rational mind can be of no other opinion.

Anselm: Therefore it is necessary that He bring to perfection what He began concerning human nature. This,
however, cannot occur, as we said, except through a
complete satisfaction for sin, which no sinner can accomplish.

Boso: I now understand that it is necessary for God to
accomplish what he has begun so as not to appear to
fail in His undertakings, for this would not be fitting.

The line which rings out is the statement "it is necessary for
God to accomplish what he has begun *so as not to appear to fail in
His undertakings,* for this would not be fitting." God's stake in the
human story did not end once the world was formed; it had only
started there. If he loved enough to create free creatures whose
destiny lay in union with himself, then in order that he should
not appear to have failed, it was fitting that he sacramentalize
the scope and depth of his love through the life, death, and
resurrection of Christ.

Creation and Resurrection:
God at the Beginning and God at the End

Christian faith understands that God lies at the beginning
of creation, calling the world into existence according to his own
creative designs. But creation is not yet finished because *we* are
not yet finished. Our particular, individual creations are still
taking place with God taking the creative and loving initiative in
our souls and through the persons and events around us by
which we are drawn to life. That is why St. Paul could write:

For the perishable must clothe itself with the imperishable, and the mortal with immortality. When the perishable has been clothed with the imperishable, and the
mortal with immortality, then the saying that is written

will come true: "Death has been swallowed up in victory" (1 Cor. 15:53–54).

And John too:

> "Father, I want those you have given me to be with me where I am, and to see my glory, the glory you have given me because you loved me before the creation of the world" (Jn. 17:24).

What finally reveals how incomplete we still are, and how unfinished is our history, and what points to the deepest meaning of creation, is the resurrection of Jesus. The resurrection is an overwhelming affirmation of life: God is always on the side of life. He desires to communicate life, he lures us to trust his way of drawing us toward life, and no matter what happens to any one of us, nothing shall separate us from the love of God if we remain faithful to his way.

The third-century Christian writer, Origen, had grasped the inner consistency of all God's actions when he explained that the resurrection of Jesus was a "type" or foreshadowing which both signified and emphasized the divine intention to create and share life. Death could never utter the final word over human history in a universe where God is the Lord of life:

> This Son, then, is also the truth and the life of all things that exist; and rightly so. For the things that were made, how could they live, except by the gift of life? Or the things that exist, how could they really and truly exist, unless they were derived from the truth? Or how could rational beings exist, unless the Word or reason had existed before them? Or how could they be wise, unless wisdom existed? But since it was to happen that some should fall away from life and bring death upon themselves by the very fact of their falling (for death is nothing else but a departure from life), and yet it would certainly not have been logical that beings once created

> by God for the enjoyment of life should utterly perish,
> it was needful that before the existence of death there
> should exist a power capable of destroying the death
> that was to come, and that there should exist a resur-
> rection, the figure of which was shown in our Lord and
> Saviour, which resurrection should have its ground in
> the very wisdom and word and life of God.

The same event which had sounded so peculiar to Paul's
Athenian audience, like an interruption of the cosmic order of
things, struck Origen as fitting and natural. Origen understood
how the resurrection was the other side of the mystery of
creation. Paul saw the resurrection as the other side of our being
made into God's children (see Acts 17:28–32).

Why did God raise Jesus from the dead? In answering this
we turn to the most original of all questions: Why did God
create the world? As Christians we believe that the Spirit which
hovered over the primordial waters was the Lord and giver of
life. It is no accident that the most solemn liturgical assembly of
the Church's year combines the resurrection celebration with
creation imagery. Holy Saturday night is replete with images of
the new beginning: the new light of Christ, the recreative waters
of baptism, the readings from the Book of Genesis, and the
triumphant Alleluias of the Risen One. For Jesus, like the first
Adam, is restored to life by the breath of God's Spirit. For us,
Christ is the key that unlocks the meaning of God's creative
designs for the world. Christ is also the sacrament of how much
God has personally invested in his creation.

Creation and Us

God stands at the beginning of creation as the one who
called the world into existence, but the fact is that our individual
experiences of being created are still taking place. This implies
that somehow each of us needs to penetrate the meaning of the
phrase "in the beginning" as it applies to us here and now.
Every day, in some sense, marks a real beginning. For God is

continually at work upon us, bringing to completion the image of Christ as it is to be traced uniquely upon each of us. On a much wider scale it can be said that creation is not yet complete because the universe itself may still be expanding. Who knows what is happening elsewhere in our galaxy, let alone in the rest of the universe? The universe too must await its perfection when the sign of Christ has been drawn across everything which exists.

When Scripture speaks about "in the beginning," we are being reminded that whatever exists depends upon God as the source and mainstay of creation. Without God, creation would be barren and sterile; it would be unable to produce anything good and permanently worthwhile which would be safe against the winds of decay. To put the matter somewhat differently, let us ask when the beginning was. Did it happen twenty billion years ago, or fifteen? Years, centuries, aeons are human measurements, and they are made because we perceive clearly that *we* had a beginning. "In the beginning" is a human and religious way of saying that we are creatures. While none of us witnessed the original moments when the cosmos exploded into an evolving universe, each of us does experience at some time or other what it means to have been created. To be a creature means to have had a beginning; it means further that we do not have the power in and of ourselves to survive forever. Life is a gift. Thus we read in the Book of Job:

> Where were you when I laid the earth's foundation?
>   Tell me, if you understand.
> Who marked off its dimensions?
>   Surely you know!
> Who stretched a measuring line across it?
> On what were its footings set, or who laid its
>   cornerstone—
>   while the morning stars sang together
>   and all the angels shouted for joy?
> Have you ever given orders to the morning
>   or shown the dawn its place? (Job 38:4–7, 12)

"In the beginning," therefore, is more than a way of introducing a report about what happened billions of years ago. It affirms a permanent relation of dependence between us and God, and it is another way of stating that God always was.

But there is a further aspect to all of this. If Christian faith knows that God stands at the front of creation, it understands further that he lies ahead of it. God sets the ultimate goal. Our thinking and speech force us to speak about "was" and "shall be." But God is as much in front of creation as behind it, as much ahead of creation as before it. If the universe is for God, then somehow he also stands at the end of things. And by "the end" I do not mean a point when the cosmic clock stops; I mean that only the one who creates can determine the reason for the universe. Only the one who creates can determine whether or not creation was successful. Why should this be the case? Because God alone sets the standard of what is finally beautiful and worthwhile, what is worth saving by uniting it with himself. We catch a glimpse of this in the resurrection of Christ.

So, in the Christian vision of things, God stands at the beginning as the one who calls the world into existence, and he stands at the end of things as the one who draws free creatures to life. John wrote:

"I am the Alpha and the Omega," says the Lord God, "who is, and who was, and who is to come, the Almighty" (Rev. 1:8).

But as the God of the living, he also stands in the middle of our history as the one who speaks, urges, and joins: "He is not the God of the dead, but of the living, for to him all are alive" (Lk. 20:38).

The overriding question which links together all the important aspects of Christian faith is: "Why does God create?" The answer to this is as simple and beautiful as it is profound and sweeping: because God loves, and out of his love he wants to communicate life.

2 People of God, People of Truth

"I am the way—and the truth and the life. No one comes to the Father except through me" (Jn. 14:6).

Most people do not spend a great deal of time discussing the nature of truth, although they will pass hours talking (and sometimes arguing) about the particular truths out of which they lead their lives. This is hardly surprising. Few of us will find much nourishment for life in abstract notions or definitions of truth. But our understanding of truth can be as concrete or abstract as our notion of God. The more real and concrete God is for us, the better do we understand what Jesus meant by identifying himself as the truth.

There are a number of specific beliefs which we hold on to and profess because they provide food for our life journey. They sustain our deepest longing to be reassured of the value of trying to lead good, upright, and faith-filled lives. We enjoy discussing and sharing those beliefs with close friends, or with someone who shows sincere interest in how we live. We will defend our beliefs against those who find little reason to believe or hope that decency and goodness are really important, or who challenge our conviction that human life is indeed a gift. Suddenly, when we are called upon to defend our beliefs, our beliefs have become "truths." The transition from belief to truth occurs as we struggle to explain why faith and life belong together.

The fact is that we cannot separate what we believe from

17

the way that we live. If we seriously hold that the earth belongs to the Lord and the fullness thereof (Ps. 24:1), then our attitude toward the earth, our lifestyle and values, will have to be affected. Being God's creatures entails certain consequences. Belief and truth, truth and life, and the desire for life and the recognition of what is true are all deeply related. This relationship runs so thoroughly through us that it accounts for who and what we are.

Indeed, truth and God belong together. How can one who is not of God recognize what is true? As Jesus said to Pilate, "For this reason I was born, and for this I came into the world, to testify to the truth. Everyone on the side of truth listens to me" (Jn. 18:37). To be on the side of truth, therefore, implies being on the side of God; but what is the nature of that intuition which joins God, life, and truth? This is the question we shall be addressing in this chapter and the next.

We shall proceed in several steps. First, we will reflect on what it means to be people of God. This is important, because our claim is that only people of God can recognize what is true. Whatever is genuinely true shows itself to be spiritual because it sustains the life of the soul. This means that whatever comes from God enhances human life, but people frequently disagree on what real human life is all about. And so we shall have to consider what is meant by the word "real" and how a Christian comes to define the term "reality." In the next chapter we will see why reality and truth tie together.

In this discussion it might be well to lay aside the problem of orthodoxy and heresy which has been surfacing in the last year or two; this is not our concern, at least not immediately. The crucial test of truth for Christians must be applied on the level of holiness of life, and that is the deeper issue in these two chapters. Let us start, therefore, by thinking for a while about what it means to be people of God.

I   ON BEING PEOPLE OF GOD

In his highly interesting little book *The Dark Interval*, John Dominic Crossan made the intriguing suggestion that the Gos-

pel story about the shepherd who rejoiced over finding his lost
sheep originated as a story about the joy of discovering the
kingdom of God. He compares this to the story of the woman
who found her lost coin.[1] By the story of the lost sheep Jesus
was implying, according to Crossan, that in order to understand
the meaning of the kingdom of God, we need to invert our
thinking: salvation is not so much a matter of God shepherding
his people as it is a matter of men and women becoming the
shepherds of God!

Crossan's suggestion echoes an idea of the twentieth-century German philosopher Martin Heidegger. In his *Letter on
Humanism* Heidegger portrayed man as the "shepherd of Being"
because to human beings falls the task of seeking, caring for,
and meditating upon Being. Responsibility for this task consti-
tutes the greatness of human nature.[2] I prefer to transpose
Heidegger's idea and say that our real greatness consists in our
capacity to know, to love, and to be transformed by God. Human beings share the responsibility of seeking, caring for, and
reflecting upon the presence of the God who is near. We also
have the task of assisting one another to notice that presence of
the God in whose image we have been made and whose voice
calls us to life.

To be people of God, in other words, is not just a way of
stating that we belong to God; it is also to realize that God in
some fashion belongs to us. We are people who have been
called to shepherd the presence of that gift which makes us
human, namely, the Spirit itself which dwells in the human heart
and draws it to life: "When you send your Spirit, they are
created, and you renew the face of the earth" (Ps. 104:30). A
human being could even be defined as "one who has been
called." Not only have we been called into existence by some
marvelous grace; we have also been called to cultivate the in-
dwelling presence of God. Our soul has been pitched to hear the
voice of that presence, and in Christ that presence receives its
proper name: he is Immanuel, God-with-us.

The God of Christian experience is a God who speaks.
Phrases like "the word of the Lord came to me" and "thus says
the Lord" occur repeatedly among the prophets of the Old

Testament. According to the opening chapters of the Book of Genesis, it is through his word that God creates. And when John wrote the familiar opening lines of his Gospel he reaffirmed that ours is not a God of mute silence, but a God of speech: "In the beginning was the Word."

God's speaking, though, is not only a sharing of information about himself; God's word carries the divine presence, for God is truly present in his word. The language that brings friends and loved ones close together is simply the language by which we become present to one another. Language and presence go together. Therefore, God's having a word helps to describe his readiness to share his presence and to communicate himself. But the Christian experience of God is located especially in the incarnation, since in this mystery the Word of God has become flesh; that Word has become present by dwelling among us, and it has dwelled among us in order to draw us toward the fullness of grace and truth.

God has spoken within our history and, as people of God, we have to listen to that history in order to hear his voice. By continually remembering that word, we shepherd our history against the ravages of meaninglessness and despair. Many have found their existence empty and vacant of meaning because they never heard the word of God clearly, or because, after hearing it, they forgot what it meant. But God's word constantly renews our existence with hope as it tells again the story of what God has done among us.

In recording the genealogy of Jesus, Matthew recalled for us the long history of God's speaking to his people. After completing the family tree of Jesus and narrating his birth, Matthew writes:

> All this took place to fulfill what the Lord had said through the prophet: "The virgin will be with child and will give birth to a son, and they will call him Immanuel"—which means, "God with us" (Mt. 1:22–23).

"All this took place": notice how Matthew has summed up the movement of history, beginning with Abraham and the establishment of Israel as the people of God. When one remembers the tales enclosed in the genealogy of Christ, the lives and fortunes which have been simply abbreviated by the mention of a name, one starts to appreciate the enormous investment of providence and grace in our history from generation to generation. "All this took place" in order that we should always be able to point to one particular event and say, "There God has spoken his word clearly and revealed to us what he is like."

Surely, the incarnation leaves no doubt about God's gracious desire to dwell among us, to share our history, and lead us into ever deeper communion with himself; the incarnation thus extends and symbolizes the mystery of our creation, and it reaffirms the dignity we enjoy in God's sight. Jesus Christ, Immanuel, God's Word made flesh, sacramentalizes the divine intention that human beings should lead lives in harmony with the Spirit within us which draws us to life and which urges us to be in harmony with one another. No instinct in Christian faith runs stronger than its conviction about God's solidarity with his people.

A philosopher might describe human thinking as the place where Being comes to presence, and a theologian might talk about the "merciful closeness of God."[3] But for the Christian, this is simply to state that God makes himself known within the human heart and in the daily business of living one's faith. Sometimes we know him as a veiled presence; sometimes we find him tabernacled in our sanctuaries. In any case, it is not God who is confined, but our attention. His mystery protects us from forgetting the source of our own holiness. God speaks to us, and his words carry his real presence; he is known, not in the way we know facts and information, but in the kind of knowing which is based on loving union.

In short, we are people of God, not just because God has taken possession of us, but because we are people whose unique possession is God. We have been called to shepherd his merciful closeness. To experience that closeness is to understand the grace of being loved and accepted for what we are.

For this reason, the reflection of Christian thinkers begins and develops within a very high realization of what being human means. Their task consists not so much in making God intelligible to the world as in rendering the world intelligible to itself. They successfully accomplish this task as men and women are helped to hear the inner voice of God and to perceive his closeness. But this is a voice and a closeness which need to be shepherded, cultivated, reflected upon, and proclaimed. For we are poor shepherds too, prone to forgetting our charge. And Christian wisdom has learned further that we neither interpret nor explain God, but it is God who interprets us. What the Lord spoke to Aaron could be applied to all of us:

> The Lord said to Aaron, "You will have no inheritance
> in their land, nor will you have any share among them;
> I am your share and your inheritance among the Israel-
> ites" (Num. 18:20).

In the same way, God's feeling for Jacob reaches to us too:

> For the Lord's portion is his people,
>   Jacob his allotted inheritance.
> In a desert land he found him,
>   in a barren and howling waste.
> He shielded him and cared for him;
>   he guarded him as the apple of his eye
>   (Dt. 32:9-10).

The First Grace

For many people, the mystery of God is of little or no concern. They rarely think about the existence of God, and if they do, they find him harmless and remote from their lives. They define themselves quite easily without referring to a human capacity for God, and it would be good to consider how this could happen.

There are matters of fact and there are matters of consequence. The claim "God exists" is quite different from the statement "Two plus two equals four" or "Washington was the first president of the United States." There is no such thing as being merely informed about God, for if one really knows that God exists, then one's living cannot remain unaffected. The statement "God exists" cannot be apprehended apart from faith, and faith makes the statement consequential. Matters of fact are understood according to the canons of reason and common sense.

The statement that God exists reports more than that there is a supreme being or a first cause; it means more than that, as a matter of fact, there is a God. The statement contains an aesthetic or a feeling about the world; one is claiming that the world which we experience makes no sense apart from God. An adequate apprehension of the existence of God, or, as Cardinal Newman put it, an assent which is not only notional but also real, requires some feeling for how the universe "fits" together. It implies a belief in the integrity of the universe, and it is based upon a perception of the order and harmony, the beauty and goodness of the world. Whenever the psalmist exclaims his wonder over the divine arrangement of created things, he is affirming the goodness and intelligibility of the world which he experiences.

The point is important. Is it possible, we might ask, for anyone to believe that God exists, that we are people who have been called to cultivate his presence in our lives, without some sentiment for the world's beauty and goodness? "God exists" lies at the center of the Christian vision of how the world shows itself. In maintaining that God exists we are expressing our belief that the world basically makes sense; we are insisting that *we* make sense because our feelings toward the world and our response to its beauty and order can be trusted as pointing to the way things are. Without being blind to the world's limitations, one can confidently say that life is good, that the universe is not a hostile place, and that people can be believed and loved. In describing the affirmation that God exists as an aesthetic judgment about the world, we are only joining forces with thinkers like Plato, Augustine, and Whitehead. Truth and beauty need to be understood together.[4]

Let me repeat the question. Can a person who does not experience the world as good and reasonable, at least sometime during his or her life, ever believe in the existence of God? Should we not say that belief in God depends so much upon experiences which invite us to praise God that without these experiences the matter of God's existence makes no sense?

The question takes us to the brink of our experience, because at stake is the integrity and justice of the universe and its Creator. The psalmist could complain:

> We are given no miraculous signs;
>> no prophets are left,
>> and none of us knows how long this will be.
> How long will the enemy mock you, O God?
>> Will the foe revile your name forever?
> Why do you hold back your hand, your right hand?
>> Take it from the folds of your garment and destroy
>> them (Ps. 74:9–11).

Many people throughout the ages could identify with the frustration of Job who had to wrestle with the injustice of life, or of the psalmist who could not fathom the slowness of God in defending his people. They resonate with the bitter disappointment of prophets who are consumed by God's word and confused by God's acts. Like John the Baptist in his prison cell, they want to ask, "Are you the one who was to come, or should we expect someone else?" (Lk. 7:20). Finally, there is the injustice of death itself, especially when it comes early or unannounced. What does the integrity of the universe mean to prophets and martyrs and people of God?

One response would be an appeal to the experience of those who have suffered and have found God in their suffering. And Christians have done this. But one is always thrown back to a prior disposition to believe, because human beings have no way of dictating the ultimate standard of justice by which to judge either God or his work. We have no way of convicting God because we have no way of determining what the successful outcome of human history should be. We are therefore tossed back to trusting and believing in God in the face of a future that we cannot see and in the face of evil that we cannot escape. Why do some people find faith while others do not?

The question needs to be treated carefully. There are some who deeply appreciate the world's beauty and grace without feeling inspired to prayers of praise and thanksgiving; they might resent being called believers. But it can be argued that whenever any of us, believer or not, rejoices over the harmony and goodness of the world and is grateful for being alive, God is surely praised. It is a compliment paid to God when one of his creatures experiences gratitude for the sheer fact of being alive to behold and marvel at the good things of this world. If such grateful spirit more or less describes a person's attitude toward life and other people, then that person is living a prayer of worship, however unspoken or incomplete it might appear to us.

What will finally judge us, both believers and unbelievers alike, is the measure of our faith. Are we convinced that the only genuinely human path through the world's injustice is the way of trust and not treachery, of love and not hatred, of patience and not anger? In one sense, every human being becomes a believer: but some believe that there is no God and the world is unordered and unjust, while others who espouse no religion lead their lives from a profound faith.

The critical moment in all this hinges, I suspect, on the development of our capacity to hear the world as calling out to us with its offers of life. We could not hear those offers unless people around us had called us to life by enabling us to believe in our own beauty, our own loveableness, and our own worth. The reasonableness and integrity of the world stand or fall with the way we perceive the meaningfulness and integrity of our own life. Our being disposed to accept the universe as the gracious place prepared for us by God depends upon whether or not we have been loved, for the mind's ability to recognize what is true is conditioned by the heart's readiness to embrace what is good. Such readiness is a grace. Since the outcome of our lives weighs on the freedom we have to love what is good, this grace is foundational. To develop the freedom to love, on which our salvation hangs, depends on someone first loving us.

What, then, is the first grace? The first grace is what becomes fundamental to everything else in human life. It is being
loved and accepted by someone before we have come to realize
and to appreciate the importance of that gift. For most people,
this gift will provide the primary example of a purely free and
gracious action on our behalf. In the context of Christian faith, it
is to know with the apostle John that God loved us first (1 Jn.
4:10), and that no one comes to the Father except through the
Son, and no one comes to the Son unless the Father first draws
him (Jn. 6:44). In the context of human relationships, it means
being grateful to parents and friends for their love. In the
context of our own solitude, first grace means being struck by
the utter gratuity of our existence; it stirs us to gladness and
gratitude for the sheer fact of being alive.

First grace is fundamental. It prefaces our entry into the
people of God. In his book *On Being a Christian*, Hans Küng
noted that the existence of God cannot be demonstrated to one
who has not found reality to be trustworthy, that is, to anyone
whose basic attitude toward the world holds human existence to
be a riddle, or an accident of evolutionary process, or simply
devoid of any intrinsic value.[5] Today, this attitude is a constant
temptation.

Other ages were more fortunate. They found the order and
harmony of the universe so obvious that their eyes lifted almost
automatically from creatures to the Creator. Thus when St.
Thomas in the thirteenth century set out to demonstrate the
existence of God by appealing to a readily observable order of
causes, and St. Bonaventure proceeded to explain how created
things could lead the soul to contemplate the glory and wisdom
of the Creator who had left his traces upon his handiwork, both
men were thinking against the profound medieval intuition
about the harmony, order, and arrangement which was so evi-
dent throughout the universe.[6]

Perhaps the hidden persuasive force of St. Anselm's argument for the existence of God, which he formulated in the
second half of the eleventh century, lies in the insight that we
cannot even think of the world without implicitly supposing that
there must be a source of order and life which makes the

existence of the world possible in the first place. In other words, the very idea of reality commits the sensitive mind to believe in the presence of God who somehow already lines the seams of our hearts and has entered the horizon of our thought and action. For St. Anselm, we do not introduce God into our world by force of rational argument because he resides there already. We cannot pivot him into the universe by "proving" his existence. God is that reality which makes meaning, value, and the reasonableness of creation possible.[7]

But we are twentieth-century Levites, and we must discharge our service to the divine presence a bit differently from saints like Anselm and Bonaventure. How does a person of today come to believe that reality is reasonable and trustworthy? This is the critical issue of the first grace; it is the presupposition for finding God in our personal histories as well as in our world. The question is settled by the personal discovery that our lives are important to other people and that what happens to us matters to them. This is one of the great challenges to catechists of any age: to help people to know their intrinsic worth. For we will be unable to admit this truth about ourselves unless we see it reflected to us by someone else's love. And this paves the road to faith:

> It is obvious that there is no greater reason either for the birth or growth of love than when one, who as yet does not love, perceives that he is loved, or when he who loves already hopes either that he may yet be loved in return, or actually has proof that he is loved. And if this holds good even in the case of base passions, how much more so in friendship? For what else do we have to be on our guard against in an offense against friendship than that our friend should think either that we do not love him, or that we love him less than he loves us? . . . Christ came chiefly for this reason, that man might learn how much God loves him, and might learn this to the end that he might begin to glow with love of Him by whom he was first loved, and so might love his neighbor at the bidding and after the example of Him

> who made Himself man's neighbor by loving him,
> when instead of being His neighbor he was wandering
> far from Him.[8]

In light of this passage, St. Augustine might have continued
by saying that a person calloused by rejection or self-hate will
never see anything beautiful about himself or the world until he
is confronted by a love which is both selfless and persistent.
Hardness of heart generates hardness of thought, but both can
be healed under the force of a love which convinces a person
that he or she is indeed good enough to love.

And what does Scripture say? Liberation theology may be
right in centering on the exodus event as central to Old Testament faith. But while the theology of liberation appeals to the
experience of deliverance as chiefly characteristic of God's action in history, perhaps the mystery of divine election needs to
be retrieved instead. For the deliverance of Israel was an accom-
plishment of God's grace; but why was God interested in Israel
in the first place? What had Israel done to merit such favor?

> For you are a people holy to the Lord your God. The
> Lord your God has chosen you out of all the peoples
> on the face of the earth to be his people, his treasured
> possession. The Lord did not set his affection on you
> and choose you because you were more numerous than
> other peoples, for you were the fewest of all peoples.
> But it was because the Lord loved you and kept the
> oath he swore to your forefathers that he brought you
> out with a mighty hand and redeemed you from the
> land of slavery (Dt. 7:6–8).

Remembering God's mighty deeds served to recall the Lord's
special affection for a small, insignificant, and wayward nation.
Prayerful attention to God's love produces the ultimate form of
deliverance, namely, the freedom to love others as the Lord has
loved us.

Why did Jesus forgive sins? Forgiveness is but the other
side of God's love, and how else could Jesus convince men and

women that God indeed loved them unless he reassured them that they were worthwhile and precious in the Father's eyes? By reaching out to touch those who had every reason to feel reject-ed, isolated, afraid, suspicious, and defeated—untouchable lep-ers, beggars in rags, outcast sinners, tax collectors, and maniacs in chains—was Jesus not in effect preparing them to realize the love of God? Was he not setting the stage for their coming to believe in God as the one who draws mercifully close in the presence of the man Jesus? The more calloused the heart, the more deprived of human acceptance and affection, the more earnestly must someone who has experienced God's love draw near to offer support, friendship, and acceptance. In precisely this way did Jesus, who experienced so profoundly the love and closeness of God, move toward others. In his very person he made really present to men and women the abiding love of his Father; this is the meaning of forgiveness.

To review: We began this section by introducing the notion of the first grace, and we did so in answer to the question about how people come to accept the statement that God exists. All of these considerations concern the general theme of being people of God.

First grace is God's gift. No matter how much we may want to pour it into someone, it remains God's to give. As freely given, it must be freely received. By this grace we come to feel at home in the universe, and with saints like Augustine and Thom-as we resonate with the harmony and beauty of the created world. By this grace we develop our ability to trust life and to notice the signs of hope which tumble around our experience and confirm the meaningfulness of human existence.

To be sure, we become signs for one another of God's presence and outreach. Having experienced his love, we mirror it forth. It shows through our eyes, in our words, and through our hands. Through our eyes God sees his world; through our hands he touches it; in our words he heals it. Nevertheless, though we compose songs about what we have experienced, dance on account of it, put it to story, describe it in psalms, write of it in theology books, speak of it to our friends in the quiet of an evening, or proclaim it by daylight with a charismatic burst of enthusiasm, that experience of God's love remains his gift. To him and to his love we can bear witness; there is nothing more we can do.

The decision for God usually unfolds slowly and undramatically in a person's life. Aroused by the living example of believers, or stirred by the restlessness in one's own heart, we come to accept, however slightly, the meaningfulness of life; we learn to trust those signs within experience which confirm our wanting to hope that there is a God who cares. The gentlest motion within the depths of the soul to believe in the integrity of creation betokens a decision for God.[9]

Such is the meaning of first grace. It cannot be explained any further. How should we explain our sense of a presence within which all of life, no matter how complicated and frustrating life might become, takes on meaning and value? How should we articulate our faith as people of God that despite the uncertainties and suffering which are part of life, we find present among us something which confers importance on everything we undertake and patiently endure—something which can be named and addressed? How should we portray that closeness which we experience, not as an escape from the brutal side of living or as a flight from insecurity, but as a closeness which can be trusted and, yes, cared for? We can do no more than tell the story of the people of God, the story of those who have learned to call that presence Immanuel, that is, God-with-us.

II THE REALITY OF LIFE AS THE REALITY OF GOD

We began this chapter by asking the question about the relation between belief and truth. At what point do we start referring to our beliefs as truths? This involves a connection between truth and life, for Christians have discovered that their beliefs are indeed life-giving, and this experience justifies our calling those beliefs true.

But there is another claim. The nature of truth is only fully grasped by people of God. When one realizes that faith in God is life-giving (God is confessed to be the Lord and giver of life), then one understands that God is the one great truth. God alone matters. And, we might add, "what matters" can serve as a short, convenient definition of reality. This is simply to follow the line of thinking about the nature of truth which was adopted by the Fourth Gospel.

In the next chapter we shall be talking directly about truth. In this section we will conclude our remarks about being people of God by considering what is meant by the term "reality."

Working Toward a Definition

What people have understood by the term "reality" has varied a great deal. For the philosopher Plato and for a number of early Christian thinkers, what were most real were ideas. Immaterial ideas, they reasoned, must have served as the pattern for the material world, and thus immaterial ideas were what mattered most in determining the shape and structure of the visible world. This intuition is liable to undergo considerable distortion, however. There are men and women who are very comfortable in their heads but who have difficulty relating to people and events in an affective way; they grow out of touch with reality as they grow less aware or expressive of their feelings. The world is excessively intellectualized.

For empirically minded people, what are most real are the objects of the senses. What matters is whatever can be touched and handled, looked at and listened to, kicked and smelled. They are in touch with their feelings but may fall into the trap of forgetting the importance of respecting one's mind. With gentle instruction, however, empiricists can be taught to notice the reality of invisible things, such as the relationships of love and friendship between people; relationships are real though invisible.

On the way to his conversion, St. Augustine reports that he could not accept the God of Christians as believable. Matter, he thought, was tainted by evil; the Christian images of God involved an incarnation, the images were necessarily inadequate to the reality of God, and anything else was impossible. Reality, Augustine reasoned, was composed of either material or immaterial "stuff," and all stuff had suffered some contamination with evil. "When I desired to think of my God," he wrote, "I could not think of Him save as a bodily magnitude—for it seemed to me that what was not such was nothing at all."[10] By confounding his understanding of reality with images of material things, Augustine was unable to conceive of that reality which was both spiritual and good. This perhaps oversimplifies his problem, but his problem demonstrates what happens when "what matters" are material things. His difficulty was complicated by the unhappy idea that evil materializes in the world and can be understood as if it were something organic. Evil, Augustine was to discover, was more like a relationship that did not succeed.[11]

In a rather different vein, and from a much later perspective, Flannery O'Connor made use of the grotesque and evil elements of human life in order to draw attention to that reality which framed the meaning of every human life, namely, divine grace. The tangibility of evil corrects the distortion of a lazy reading of the human story and the diminished sense of what is real. She wrote:

> I suppose the reasons for the use of so much violence in modern fiction will differ with each writer who uses it, but in my own stories I have found that violence is strangely capable of returning my characters to reality and preparing them to accept their moment of grace. Their heads are so hard that almost nothing else will do the work. This idea, that reality is something to which we must be returned at considerable cost, is one which is seldom understood by the casual reader, but is one which is implicit in the Christian view of the world.

And then, commenting on one of her own short stories, she added:

> This story has been called grotesque, but I prefer to call it literal. A good story is literal in the same way that a child's drawing is literal. When a child draws, he doesn't intend to distort but to set down exactly what

he sees, and as his gaze is direct, he sees the lines that
create motion. Now the lines of motion that interest the
writer are usually invisible. They are lines of spiritual
motion.[12]

For this Catholic writer, therefore, "what matters" was neither
ideas nor things, nor evil for its own sake; "what matters" was
the inner, spiritual moment of grace.

Perhaps the most influential modern thinker on the problem of reality and how we come to know it was the eighteenth-
century philosopher Immanuel Kant. For Kant, what is most real
is simply not accessible to human understanding; reality therefore reduces to whatever appears to us. But whatever appears to
us must first pass through our senses. Between our senses on
the one hand, and certain structures of the mind on the other
hand, we are prevented from grasping reality as it is "in itself."
Thus Kant had distinguished reality as appearance from reality
as it truly is, and then concluded that what truly is cannot be
known, at least by reason.

This formulation yielded distressing results, for it placed
"what matters" outside the scope of critical thinking and it
estranged God from the inner dynamics of thought, feeling, and
experience. Modern theology has been afflicted with the Kant-
ian legacy, I believe, in the way in which it has uncritically
accepted the task of distinguishing between the Jesus of history
(reality as it is in itself) and the Christ of faith (reality as
apparent to the early Church and to us). The faith of some
believers ran aground on philosophical shoals as they tackled
the problem of discovering the "real" Jesus Christ and were
unable to locate him.

At any rate, there have been many opinions about what
reality is.

I recall once sitting on a stone wall just at the edge of a
village in India, watching the various activities in the villagers'
daily routine. Some were stooping to plant rice seedlings in the
small paddies of a nearby field; a few were tending to the goats
and chickens; some women were washing clothes at the pond or
drawing water from the village well; some were preparing

food—I could hear the spattering and sizzling of cooking oil coming from somewhere; others were squatting outside a mud hut and chatting. The entire scene brimmed with life, like a Brueghel painting in an Asian setting. Although I was actually quite useless in the midst of the energy and effort going on around me, I was struck by how "real" that village seemed. Things mattered there.

Remembering the scene, and my experience in it, invites a reflection. Sometimes in the business of life we can be bothered by a dull sensation that our work and concerns are not real; they seem thin and unimportant. At other times we experience situations which strike us as important, where what is happening around us is fraught with meaning, yet at the same time we feel like powerless bystanders. Some have experienced this in watching a person die. These moments summon us to reflect about what matters in life; our growing to new life depends on how we answer the summons. The meaning of reality cannot be discussed fruitfully apart from those experiences which promote life by teaching us about what truly matters.

One scriptural text is particularly helpful in pointing to the connection between reality and life:

> See, I set before you today life and prosperity, death and destruction. For I command you today to love the Lord your God, to walk in his ways, and to keep his commands, decrees, and laws; then you will live and increase, and the Lord your God will bless you in the land you are entering to possess.... I have set before you life and death, blessings and curses. Now choose life, so that you and your children may live and that you may love the Lord your God, listen to his voice, and hold fast to him. For the Lord is your life (Dt. 30:15–16, 19–20).

If reality is understood in terms of what is life-giving, and, as the text suggests, if life is supposed to be understood in terms of God and his ways, then reality and God are intimately connected. We can illustrate the nature of this connection with a classic example.

A fascinating piece of writing from the fourth century is St. Athanasius' account of the life of Antony of the Desert.[13] As a young man, while daydreaming one day about what it might have been like to be walking in the company of Jesus and his disciples, Antony was struck by the desire to devote his life to seeking God above all things. Portrayed against the background of the barren desert wastes, Antony's life was one of intense thirst. His soul ached for God as the parched desert sand would soak up the rain. Into the deepest part of the desert he journeyed, and then up a mountain and into its inner recesses: Antony's physical journey reflected the inward travels of a soul into the solitary places where one stands alone with God.

He waged war with demons. Threatened by the presence of someone who wanted to inhabit and domesticate their wild haunts, the demons hounded Antony with all sorts of disguises and torments. They came as wolves, scorpions, and snakes. When he wanted to pray, they urged him to sleep; when he wanted to sleep, they tempted him to prayer. But after years of hardship, thirst, fasting, and prayer, Antony appeared as strong, healthy, and calm as a young man rising from sleep. His search for God left him more joyous, more alive, and freer than ever before. What had taken place?

According to Athanasius, Antony had learned to distinguish between good and evil spirits; he had become skilled in the ways of God. In the years of experiencing and reflecting upon the conflicting movements in his soul, Antony mastered the art of discernment. He could distinguish the desires which were life-giving from other desires which, like a mirage on the sand, promised much but delivered nothing.

In his "Notes for a Philosophy of Solitude," Thomas Merton remarked that each one's desert must be designated by the finger of God.[14] The desert symbolizes that inner ground or frontier where each person must make the choice for life. The desert is that space where we come face to face with the unsettled part of ourselves and where, like Antony, we learn to let ourselves be led by the deepest of all desires, the desire for life. For the person of faith God alone is the Lord and giver of life, and therefore the desire for life is in fact the desire for God. "Thou didst touch me," wrote St. Augustine, "and I have burned for thy peace."

Discerning What Is Real

Many things compete with the desire for life. The false claimants appear—money, possessions, reputation, cosmetics, entertainment—all promising to provide what belongs to God alone to give. "I have set before you life and death, blessings and curses," Moses reminded the people. "For the Lord is your life." The wisdom gained from each one's desert-experience is knowledge of the ways of God. In the desert God himself is both teacher and guide, the cloud by day and the pillar of fire by night. "There are two Ways, one of Life and one of Death, and there is a great difference between the two Ways." So wrote that early Christian who authored the *Didache*.[15] Choose life, he advised; choose the things which are truly life-giving, since they are of God.

The moral prescriptions which the *Didache* enjoined on those catechumens who were about to enter upon the way of the Gospel through baptism represent Christian wisdom. For the people of God had learned that certain things are right (and therefore to be urged) while other things are wrong (and thus to be avoided) because what is right will eventually prove life-giving, and what is evil can only produce death. This is what is represented by the Ten Commandments, or by the baptismal sermons of the early Church Fathers who were so thoroughgoing in their review of the moral obligations assumed at baptism; it is recalled in the present baptismal inquiry, "Do you reject Satan? And all his works? And all his empty promises?"

Antony learned to detect the evil spirit because it brought anxiety, confusion, loud noises, distraction, boredom, doubt, uncertainty, and fear. The person seduced by this spirit could easily wind up eaten by selfishness, narrow-mindedness, and suspicion; he would appear hateful, threatened, and prematurely dead. The good spirit, on the contrary, was manifested by peace, freedom, trust, confidence, inner quiet, joy, and a consciousness of the needs of one's neighbor. The person alive to this spirit becomes more open, trusting, capable of selfless service, reverent, and humble. As the desire for life unfolds in the faithful seeking of God above all else, the desert teaches that fidelity to one's deepest self—the self that longs for God—will lead to the experience of a richer life. It is hardly surprising that the prophets reminded the people of Israel that the moments when they really came to know God occurred, not in the safety of their defense treaties, nor in the splendor of temple and cult, nor in times of prosperity. The moments of real knowing took place in the wilderness. "Therefore I am now going to allure her; I will lead her into the desert and speak tenderly to her" (Hos. 2:14).

The desire for life is often displaced onto lesser goods. "Seek first the kingdom of God," Jesus instructed his disciples, "and everything else will be given to you." In the way of wisdom, which is frequently the way of the desert, one learns that creatures which parade in the name of God can never give life. The demon, like the desert's mirage, is a liar. "Among all the temptations wherewith he tempted St. Antony," Francis Thompson wrote, "though we have often seen it stated that he howled, we have never seen it stated that he sang."[16] The demon is no musician either.

What, Then, Is Reality?

Our concern in this section has been to explain that reality, life, and God are related. The question about reality has not been raised in order to satisfy a speculative interest in philosophical ideas; our interest lies in the meaning of Scripture. The living God enjoined his people to choose the way of life. In summoning them to faith and trust, God was simply calling the people to life as they discovered what truly matters. Human beings are alive and real as they grow to be people of faith and people of God.

Frequently we oppose what is real to what is imaginary.

"Real" denotes the concrete, tangible things around us which can be perceived through the senses. But this does not exhaust the meaning of the term. Reality includes more than the assorted objects around us like tables and chairs, cars and televisions, clothes and food, books and tennis rackets. Reality even includes more than objects plus people. To be blessed with material things and other people around us is not enough to immunize us against boredom, loneliness, and emptiness. Reality and life are inseparable. Reality is what matters for life; it is gauged by the quality of our living, by our involvement with others, by internal freedom and peace, and by fidelity to the way of the Lord. Our lives take on a taste of unreality when, despite the activities and concerns which occupy us, life itself gets affectively narrow and unengaging.

Consequently, reality is neither a thing nor the sum total of things, nor is it things plus human beings thrown in for good measure. Reality is not thing-like. Reality is better described in terms of friendship, being touched and loved, fidelity to commitments, awareness of the wider needs and hopes of the human family, and perseverance in faith.

Essentially, then, reality is not a matter of correct ideas but of the concerns and feelings which locate us in life. The threat of existing in an unreal and unauthentic manner requires continual vigilance. For as we perceive ourselves less involved in what is happening in the world around us, less alert to the needs of others, less compassionate toward those afflicted with moral blindness, and as we find ourselves more or less bored with life, incapable of being moved by the world's beauty, and more withdrawn into our own shells, then it is time to ask what is happening inside of us, what our feelings are saying, where life is slipping away, and where the reality-loss is occurring.

Christian faith confesses that God is the ultimately real One, the true source of meaning, value, and life. Creation matters to God; creation is real for him; his feelings of love and compassion for us are genuine. The call to faith, that is, the call to believe in the goodness of creation and the providence of God, to trust that our desire for life will not be ultimately frustrated, and to cooperate with that desire by moving outside of ourselves in love for one another, is indeed the call to life. To desire life and to know that reality in which we can come to life is simply to desire God and to perceive the world through faith in him.

Reality, like life, is never exhausted by a definition. Neither can we ever have a handle on God, sum him up, or reduce him to our expectations and ideas. The presence of God is associated with actions, thoughts, or situations which are genuinely life-giving. Even in the midst of suffering we can notice God's presence if what we are experiencing reveals "lines of spiritual motion." The evil we endure will forge and simplify life if our suffering is joined to a basic trust in God, the Lord who has chosen to be among us even in pain, diminishment, and death.

To review: The Christian wisdom of people like Antony of the Desert knew how to answer the question "What is real?" because the desert-experience schooled them in the ways of God. The desert teaches the lesson that God alone is real, and that we are real in the measure that we are people of God.

NOTES

1. John Dominic Crossan, *The Dark Interval: Towards a Theology of Story* (Chicago, 1975), pp. 96–101.

2. See Martin Heidegger, *Basic Writings* (New York, 1977), pp. 189–242.

3. Rahner employs this idea frequently in *Foundations of Christian Faith: An Introduction to the Idea of Christianity* (New York, 1978).

4. On the importance of this point for understanding Augustine, see Robert J. O'Connell, S.J., *Art and the Christian Intelligence in St. Augustine* (Cambridge, Mass., 1978). On Whitehead, see Donald W. Sherburne, *A Whiteheadian Aesthetic* (Hamden, Conn., 1970).

5. Hans Küng, *On Being a Christian* (New York, 1976), pp. 62–88.

6. For St. Thomas' case, see *Summa Contra Gentiles,* Book One, Chapter 13, trans. Anton C. Pegis (Notre Dame, Ind.,

1975). For Bonaventure's case, see *The Soul's Journey into God*, trans. Ewert Cousins (New York, 1978).

7. For this appreciation of the ontological argument, I am indebted to Edward Husserl's notion of appresence as it is discussed by Edward Farley in *Ecclesial Man: A Social Phenomenology of Faith and Reality* (Philadelphia, 1975), Chapter 9.

8. St. Augustine, *The First Catechetical Instruction*, trans. Joseph P. Christopher (New York: Paulist Press), pp. 22–23.

9. The idea is taken from Karl Rahner. See, for instance, his essay "Anonymous Christians" in *Theological Investigations*, Volume 6 (New York, 1974). See also *Foundations of Christian Faith*, pp. 24–91.

10. St. Augustine, *The Confessions*, trans. F.J. Sheed (Kansas City, 1970), p. 80.

11. *The Confessions*, Book 7:12, pp. 118–119.

12. Flannery O'Connor, *Mystery and Manners* (New York, 1979), pp. 112–113.

13. St. Athanasius, *The Life of Antony and the Letter to Marcellinus*, trans. Robert C. Gregg (New York, 1980).

14. Thomas Merton, "Notes for a Philosophy of Solitude," *Disputed Questions* (New York, 1976), pp. 163–193.

15. The *Didache* (or, The Teaching of the Twelve Apostles) dates from the late first or early second century. The text can be found in various places. See, for example, *The Apostolic Fathers*, trans. Kirsopp Lake (Cambridge, Mass., 1970).

16. Francis Thompson, *Shelley* (London, 8th edition, 1923), pp. 69–70.

3 On Being
People of Truth

In the previous chapter we tried to show that the life of God is the vital center of Christian experience; what is of God determines what is real for us. Reality and faith, then, are not two opposing ideas. Faith and reality are linked by their common relationship to life. Faith, we might say, arises both from God's call to life and from the grace which enables us to respond to his call day by day. Reality, we have seen, consists of "what matters" as we grow fully alive. St. Paul said the same thing, much more simply, in his Letter to the Romans:

> Those who live according to their sinful nature have their minds set on what that nature desires; but those who live in accordance with the Spirit have their mind set on what the Spirit desires. The mind of the sinful man is death, but the mind controlled by the Spirit is life and peace (Rom. 8:5–6).

Now it is time to notice that truth is known on the basis of whatever proves to be life-giving, and as God is the source of life, he is also the ultimate truth.

Understanding the Idea of Truth

Just as the terms "reality" and "life" need to be enriched by faith, so also does the notion of truth. When John records Jesus

41

as saying, "I am the way and the truth and the life" (Jn. 14:6), he surely has more in mind than a correct proposition. This truth is more than verbal; it refers to the truth which Jesus is. This truth is personal, and it relates to life. By following Jesus, his disciples throughout the centuries have come to understand the meaning of John's words: "But these things are written that you may believe that Jesus, is the Christ, the Son of God, and that by believing you may have life in his name" (Jn. 20:31).

The call to faith, which is also the call to life, is necessarily a call to truth. In short, the great truth given to Christians was Jesus Christ. He was neither an abstract principle nor a great idea, neither a philosophy nor a worldview. Jesus Christ was the concretely historical person in whose company believers lived, a person to be known, contemplated, and loved. Jesus, the truth of God, appears on the pages of the Gospels and dwells through the Spirit in human hearts. Christian saints would be astonished to hear that truth ultimately could be anything other than personal.

Various Senses of the Word

The word "truth" has been employed in at least three senses. First, truth sometimes designates correct statements about the world, about the way things are, or about events which have happened. In this sense, truth means making correct statements about matters of fact. There is usually no point to arguing over matters of fact; it is over the interpretation of facts and events that people disagree.

There is a deeper sense, however. Truth sometimes refers to one's intention, that is, to the meaning that lies behind the words, sentences, and expressions which we use. Realizing this, before we accuse someone of having made a mistake or of telling a lie, we ask whether we have understood his words aright. A mistake, of course, is one thing. But to catch someone in a lie means that we have gone beyond his words and located a motive. It is to spot a planned contradiction between language and thought. Language should reflect a willingness to reveal and to share, but a lie represents the will to conceal and to deceive. The liar does violence to language.

In this second sense of the word "truth," therefore, being truthful describes a person whose speech does not hide what he or she is. Rather, such speaking is anchored in an openness, freedom, and trust; it is free and trusting because one has no reason to be afraid for what he is or for what he does. As Jesus taught in the Sermon on the Mount, "Simply let your 'Yes' be 'Yes,' and your 'No,' 'No' " (Mt. 5:37). A truthful person has no need to take an oath; his speech can be trusted.

Being truthful does not guarantee that one is always correct. In fact, there are numerous occasions when correct knowledge is far more crucial than sincerity. Being truthful simply means that a truthful person has nothing to hide and that this freedom underlies one's thinking and living. To draw an obvious point, we can ask: Is it not the case that Christian faith knows God to be utterly truthful because, having nothing to hide or to lose, God reveals himself for what he is? This divine freedom is suggested by the Fourth Gospel's portrayal of God as having a Word which became flesh and which witnessed to the Father's love. The God who spoke that word is truthful because he is free.

But there is a third sense of the word "truth." Besides referring to the content of what is said, or to the integrity of the speaker, truth may designate something which has to be lived out and not merely intellectually accepted. And so the Church proposes the doctrines or mysteries of faith as truths to be believed. In this context, truth relates to life insofar as truth penetrates our thinking, feeling, imagining, and relating to others; not only is truth put into practice, but practice is also shaped by the truth. Truth then functions as a call to life, inviting us forward to a deeper faith, a stronger hope, and a quicker love.

The twentieth-century philosopher Alfred North Whitehead remarked that it is more important for propositions to be interesting than for propositions to be true.[1] Whitehead did not define truth in the senses I have suggested here, but what he said points to the idea of truth defined as a call. What is interesting and beautiful can move the mind to reflect, and such reflection can influence the direction of our living. Truth evokes a change of heart by appealing to our desire for life and by persuasively drawing us to pursue what is life-giving. The call of truth, like the call of faith, is a call to life. The truth of the Gospel, the truth which Jesus is, attracts us because it interests our heart; its beauty calls out to us.

St. John recounts Jesus praying at the Last Supper that his disciples should receive the Spirit of truth (Jn.14:17) and that they should abide in his Father's word, which is truth (Jn. 17:16). John's concern for truth represents something far more serious than a preoccupation with correct information. Jesus is the truth, and truth apparently initiates a distinctive spiritual logic: truth leads to freedom (Jn. 8:32), freedom leads to peace (Jn. 14:26–27), peace leads to joy (Jn. 15:11), joy is founded in love (Jn. 15:9–10), and love leads to union, the chief mark or proof of Jesus' disciples (Jn. 17:11, 20–23). The call to truth, to faith, and to life, is existentially characterized by the special gifts of the Spirit—peace, freedom, joy, love, and union. Such gifts testify to the Gospel's truth.

Truth Versus Correctness

Few people talk seriously about the "truth" of geography or the "truths" of science. In these areas it is enough to say that we are talking about matters of fact or correct knowledge. I think it is helpful to distinguish truth from correctness so that the notion of truth will stand as enriched as possible. No one is expected to live out the facts of science or geography. But when we hear someone talking about the truth of the Gospel, we understand that more is intended than the mere fact that Jesus was born, or the fact that he lived in Palestine, or the fact that he was a young man when he died. At stake is his significance for us. Our ability to grasp the meaning of what he is and what he has done continues to grow and percolate through the many dimensions and stages of our lives. The significance of Jesus for

us brings us to pray over the facts of his life. The truth which
Jesus is both calls and attracts, challenges and transforms.

The truth of the Gospel, then, is a living truth, for the
Gospel makes no sense unless and until it is lived. In itself the
Gospel's truth does not change; we are changed in living it. The
community of believers in whom truth resides and who thus
dwell in the truth will change and develop as they respond to the
call to life. Like reality, like God himself, truth in this enriched
sense is never summed up and defined in a book; the truth of
the Gospel lives and grows in us as we live and grow in it. Such
is the beautiful meaning of Paul's words that we should put on
the mind of Christ, and of Paul's realization, "I no longer live,
but Christ lives in me" (Gal. 2:20). As the apostle John knew, all
the statements and all the books in the world would not adequately contain the truth about Christ (Jn. 20:30–31). This kind
of truth always outstrips its verbal casings.[2]

Correcting a Wrong Impression

There is a common misconception about truth, and we
cannot conclude our discussion of truth without addressing it.
Many people seem to think that somewhere there exists an
absolute standard of correctness against which all human knowledge can be measured to see whether it is right. This idea is
mistaken. It is like attempting to conceive of "the real me." But
in what timeless heaven does the "real" me exist? Who is the
real me? Could it be the self I was ten years ago? The self I am
today? What I shall be like in twenty years? And if I should die
sooner than I counted on, will the real me remain forever
unrealized? Clearly, there is no perfect, ideal self. There is
simply this plain, everyday bundle of nerves, desires, ideas, and
heart which begins each day with fresh intention and ends its
day with some sorrow, some gratitude, and much hope.

Certainly, there is a large body of widely accepted knowledge to which we subscribe as intelligent people. But what does
that body of knowledge represent? What does all that information add up to? It represents the answers which have satisfied

the questions of innumerable scientists, researchers, inventors, thinkers, and scholars. All knowledge and all human science are built up from the kind of questions it occurs to someone to ask.

What then is correctness all about? Consider an example. In the process of learning, a teacher's job is to generate the right questions in the mind of a student, a job which usually demands imagination and creativity. In general, answers will not appear important and will not be remembered for very long unless they come in response to one's personal questioning. If a student does not want to understand, if he cannot get inside of a question and with his mind feel what the question means, then the student will not learn; he can only memorize information. A good teacher wants students to be intrigued enough to wonder, to raise their hands and ask other questions, to think, and to discover for themselves.

The idea of correctness arises as we catch the connection between questions and the answers which satisfy them. If we raise intelligent questions and make strategic insights, then we shall discover the "right" answers. Questions are frequently more interesting than their corresponding answers, especially in areas like theology, literature, history, and philosophy, because they reveal the concerns which people have about themselves and about the world. Human knowledge, no matter what field one is engaged in, cannot avoid reflecting the concerns, the interests, and the backgrounds of individuals and societies. Knowledge does not exist until human beings start to raise questions.[3] The human race boasts an enormous amount of correct knowledge.

But truth is something else. Truth usually has moral and religious tones, and what many people find unsettling is the implication that truth is relative and purely subjective. They fear that there may be no way of reaching certitude over their beliefs; they want to be sure that their beliefs are correct. Ecclesiastical authority might help to safeguard their beliefs against uncertainty, and they will cling to that authority until it becomes obvious that authorities are also capable of making mistakes.

Still, with some reflection it is possible to see that truth is always subjective, since it exists in human minds; and truth is always relative, since men and women come to understand truth with varying degrees of insight and from wide-ranging differences of perspective. Belief in God, for example, is just a bottom line affirmation, a starting point. To be fruitful, that belief needs to breathe with us; it has to penetrate our desires and our entire way of life. Truth can only be truth in the proper sense when it functions as a call upon us, that is, when it becomes subjective. Truth is relative in that people take possession of it and grow in it, some very much, some just a little, and some not at all (see Mk. 4:1-20 on the parable of the sower). If a belief exercises no more influence than the number of moons around Jupiter, then we are dealing, not with truth, but with information which happens to be correct. Indeed, in this regard truth is always both subjective and relative. Correct beliefs are successful only if they aim men and women toward God.

To view the issue from another side, we might observe that the doctrines of our creed are also called the truths of faith. The creed spells out what Christian faith is. To omit one of those doctrines, to substitute something else in its place, or to understand it in a sense different from what the common mind of the Church means by that doctrine would amount to an incorrect grasp of Christian faith. It would be similar to changing the rules of a game when a particular play is desirable but forbidden. The creed embraces the great Christian facts, and to change the facts is to fail to play by the rules.

But the doctrines of faith are also known as mysteries, both because they have been divinely revealed and because they are truths. As truths, they are intended to live in the believer's soul. Or rather, as truths they summon the soul to the fullness of life. Those who worry that their beliefs may not be right or correct have to be instructed to see that not every religious doctrine or practice is indeed life-giving. There are obstacles along the path; there are false gods. Yet as Christians, we believe the truths of our faith and trust the moral wisdom of the people of God. The Church does not possess an abstract norm of correctness which it consults to obtain absolute certainty, nor can it boast of impeccable authorities. Being people of God means letting ourselves be drawn by the Spirit of Christ, so that we become people of truth. We believe the truths of faith because they have proven themselves to be a way of life. They have been verified throughout the history of the Christian community and in our personal experience by the accompanying fruits of the Spirit.[4]

Conclusion

The overall theme of these two chapters has been the relationship between being people of God and being people of truth. We started by raising a question about why we insist that what we believe as Christians must also be true. This led to our considering what it means to be people of God, the first grace through which we are enabled to accept the reality of God and the nature of reality. The whole discussion turns on the desire for life and the need to discern what is life-giving, for from this comes our grasp of the nature of truth.

In the last few years, we have heard a great deal about theologians causing trouble with novel and possibly heretical ideas. But beneath the flurry of words between Church authorities and some theologians there lies the deeper issue of how the people of God recognize truth in the first place. Part of the difficulty has been verbal, that is, it has been a problem of finding words to express ancient beliefs in ways that make sense to people of our day. The underlying issue, however, is a spiritual one, for any genuine truth has power to move and nourish the life of the soul.

However, I do not think it unreasonable to maintain that no authority, ecclesiastical or theological, can move our souls; only the truth can stir us. The fact that we find ourselves moved by a belief or by the words of Scripture should be a clue that the truth is taking over us. And if our belief leads us to a richer spiritual life—more joyous, more free, more eager to bear one another's burdens, and so on—then the genuineness of the truth is attested to by the presence of the Spirit. After all, the authority of truth is not guaranteed by the truthfulness of authority nor the integrity of theology; these can only point to it.

The authority of truth is guaranteed finally by the Spirit of God, and this Spirit is recognized by those who are on God's side.

There is an absolute standard of truth, just as there is something which is ultimately real: and this is God. It is the God who made Adam, who called Moses from the burning bush, who loved the world enough to join its history, the God called by the name which, Matthew recalled, came through an angel's announcement: Immanuel. By devoutly contemplating Christ, the Christian understands why reality, truth, and life are summed up once and for all in Jesus.

When all is said and done, there is only God. We are a people gradually learning about the image in which we have been fashioned. Our God abides among us, drawing us together in himself, renewing us in his image (Col. 3:11). We live, as it were, in God's neighborhood. Truth is what we are becoming, however imperceptibly the God-life in us seems to be growing. Truth is also what we are, however meager our holiness might seem to us. And truth is recognized as what gives life, funding our sense of what is real and worthwhile. Truth is the God who comes mercifully close, and we are the people who have been called to dwell in the presence of that truth which alone matters.

NOTES

1. See Alfred North Whitehead, *Adventures of Ideas* (New York, 1967), p. 244. The notion of truth as a call is also quite Heideggerian. See, for example, Martin Heidegger, *What Is Called Thinking?* (New York, 1968).

2. For a lengthy treatment of the Johannine understanding of truth, see Ignace de la Potterie, S. J., *La Vérité dans Saint Jean,* 2 volumes (Rome, 1977).

3. I owe this view of truth and correctness to a number of readings of Bernard Lonergan, *Insight: A Study of Human Understanding* (London and New York, 1957).

4. On the nature of tradition as grounding the validity of moral wisdom, see Hans-Georg Gadamer, *Truth and Method* (New York, 1975), p. 249.

4 Growing To Be People of God

One of the most beautiful chords which plays insistently in the writings and sermons of the early Church Fathers is that the Son of God became a son of man in order that we, the sons and daughters of men, might have the power to become children of God. For the early Christians, the incarnation symbolized that marvelous and mysterious display of God's freedom whereby he determined to become part of his creatures' history.

The freedom of God is the key phrase here. The compassion and forgiveness which marked the ministry of Jesus were but the other side of God's own freedom. For only one who is free can truly forgive; only one who is empty of self is free enough to be compassionate in the face of ingratitude and hatred. "Father, forgive them, for they do not know what they are doing" (Lk. 23:34). If being compassionate depends upon being free—free of self-love, of pride, even of a hold on one's own life—then our becoming sons and daughters of God has to involve our growth in genuine freedom.

The Spirit of Christ can empower us to become like Christ; the same Spirit empowered Christ to be like the Father. In becoming free we become compassionate; in being compassionate we become perfect; in being merciful we become like God. With St. Matthew it is to say, "Be perfect, therefore, as your heavenly Father is perfect" (Mt. 5:48), and with St. Luke, "Be merciful, just as your Father is merciful" (Lk. 6:36).

Becoming free, however, is no simple achievement. We do

50

not become compassionate merely by willing to be free of self-love. For we can fairly easily *do* good things if we set our minds to do them. But only with God's grace will we spontaneously and regularly *think* good thoughts toward and about other people. Our deeper reactions tend to be more or less involuntary, and these involuntary reactions may provide a decent (though perhaps disappointing) reading of precisely how far our hearts are turned toward God. The Lord's attitude toward us is spontaneously compassionate, a characteristic which we may find difficult to fathom:

> "For my thoughts are not your thoughts, neither are
> your ways my ways," declares the Lord. "As the heav-
> ens are higher than the earth, so are my ways higher
> than your ways and my thoughts than your thoughts"
> (Is. 55:8–9).

How then do we grow in those deep, recessive, and unfree regions of our hearts? How are those regions to be reformed which resist our consciously willed efforts to change them? How is genuine compassion learned? Perhaps, as Jesus suggested, only by prayer and fasting. Perhaps only by prayerful, regular attention to the example of Christ, that is, by daily and intimate familiarity with the ways of God. We become free by contemplating the freedom of God. And that means listening to what God wants to say about himself.

In the first chapter we were considering God's investment in creation, and in the second and third chapters we were concerned with the way Christians come to know what is true out of their experience of God. In this chapter we shall describe a few dimensions of that experience, and the reader will have to judge whether my description rings true.

A Story about Friendship

People need parks and gardens to walk in in order to touch their thoughts and feelings through a few moments of solitude. That is why God created Adam in a garden. Adam grew out of the earth, and so the earth was to be a permanent reminder of his creaturehood and the gift of spirit which breathed through his body.

The first few pages of the Bible intimate a picture of God and Adam walking in a park or garden. The evening draws on, and we might imagine that God has an arm around Adam's shoulder. They are chatting, one friend with another, and the Lord points with obvious pleasure to the garden's most recent additions. He asks Adam how he likes them.

One evening God enters the park, but Adam is not there. God calls, "Adam, where are you?" But the only sound to be heard is the wind rustling through the leaves. Centuries pass, and God still comes to the garden at evening, looking for Adam. And hearing no sound, he walks through the park with great sadness, lonely for the friendship and intimacy of the one who could enjoy his company—Adam, his first created son. And Adam, I suppose the story would go, has wandered far over the earth, feeling guilty and confused but no longer sure for what reason. He has long since forgotten about those evenings among the hedgerows and fruit-bearing trees, although gardens and parks can still trigger feelings of lost companionship. Adam too carries a deep loneliness for the God with whom he was once so familiar. Adam, of course, is us; Adam is the whole human race.

I have sometimes found myself swinging slowly in a park bench as the stars begin to dot the summer sky, experiencing a little loneliness myself, and wondering if all loneliness does not share in the loneliness of God longing for Adam. Until the human family rediscovers the God who desires to be close to us, God too will be lonely. Until that time, all human loneliness takes its bittersweet taste from the feelings which God has toward the world. I say "bittersweet" because in the experience of loneliness there lurks the distant memory and the faint wish that things should be otherwise. We are created for communion. Having once known intimacy and friendship, it is hard to live without them. We are made for each other, and we are made to be in union with the Lord. ·

Christian faith understands this truth. In the incarnation,

we do not see God striking up a friendship with the human race for the second time, as it were; we do not behold the face of a hostile God whose attitude toward us changes as he looks upon his Son walking on the earth. The incarnation is not the mystery of God tearing through the distance between us and him. Rather, in Christ God displays his compassionate closeness; he discloses a reconciliation and friendship that belong between us and himself from the time of Adam.

Enlarging Our View of God

Some people may be uncomfortable over the suggestion that God could be lonely. God, they would urge, is changeless, timeless, and self-sufficient; he enjoys a constant communion within the life of the Trinity. As the fourth preface for weekdays in ordinary time reads, "You have no need of our praise, yet our desire to praise you is itself your gift." Whenever the Bible depicts God as angry, delighted, jealous, or disappointed, these people regularly interpret those divine feelings as anthropomorphic. They do not, surprisingly, explain God's love as a projection of human feeling onto God. It is difficult for them to entertain the idea that God could really desire anything.

On the other hand, a moment's reflection on our prayer life would probably reveal an experience of a God who is anything but passive or lacking in feeling. The way that we speak to God and the things we expect of him presuppose a God who is active, concerned, and continually responding to us with feeling.

For example, suppose we are going to ask God for a favor. If God already knows what he will do, and if he is changeless, then our prayer is not going to induce God to change his mind. What point is there in petitioning him? Furthermore, if we really trusted him, we should have no reason to ask God for anything. Whatever happens to us only occurs with his knowledge and providential consent.

Is it possible that a prayer of petition actually indicates a failure to trust in God's love? Is there any point in our requesting something from the Lord unless he simply enjoys being asked for things which he is already prepared to bestow? Indeed, there are times when our request signals a lack of trust, as Peter discovered:

> "Lord, if it's you," Peter replied, "tell me to come to you on the water."
>
> "Come," he said.
>
> Then Peter got down out of the boat and walked on the water to Jesus. But when he saw the wind, he was afraid and, beginning to sink, cried out, "Lord, save me!"
>
> Immediately Jesus reached out his hand and caught him. "You of little faith," he said, "why did you doubt?" (Mt. 14:28–31).

There is something consoling about the possibility that God enjoys our asking him for his blessing, as one friend enjoys another's expression of familiarity and need. Thus Jesus instructed his disciples by his teaching and his example to pray to God as their Father, the very one who knows their needs even before they ask him (Mt. 6:8), who knows how to give good gifts to his children (Lk. 11:13), and who loves and hears the disciples because they love his Son (Jn. 16:26–27).

We believe, of course, that in his love God would no more withhold what is for our good than he would set out to hurt us. But what is going on when we stand before the Lord in petitioning him?

It is true that God does not change; he is not changed by our praying to him. But God's being changeless does not mean that he is either immobile, unconcerned, or set in his ways. What is our experience? Is it not the case that we would come to pray only with great reluctance unless we knew God to be personally active, involved, and in love with us? We do not have to beg God to take an interest in our lives or in our world; he already has an investment in our fortunes. As the Creator, God draws the world to that purpose for which he made it. God desires to communicate his own life to us who are the work of his hands; it is his goodness which is changeless.

All Christian prayer proceeds from the conviction that if

our intention is joined to God's, then we shall not be asking him for something he is unwilling to give. "Thy will be done," we pray, for we respect his larger designs for us and the whole human race. God moves actively in every circumstance of life, even if we do not see how, in order to draw us further into his life.

To sum up, then, we can say that Christian prayer supposes a God who is active and concerned about his people. He is changeless in his desire to communicate life and thus faithful to his reason for creating the world. Through our prayer *we change* as we grow more aware of our dependence upon God for life; *we change* as our desires become purified and our outlook is joined closely to the Lord's. Prayer readies the way for deeper faith and for our ability to find God in whatever happens to us. Personally, I hope that God does feel how intensely I want certain things, but I also hope that what I desire is precisely what the Lord desires; and for that reason, I believe he moves them along. "And we know," wrote St. Paul, "that in all things God works for the good of those who love him, who have been called according to his purpose" (Rom. 8:28).

Sharing in God's Experience

As Christians, much of our personal growth in freedom takes place in contemplating the freedom of God, that is, the freedom out of which he made the world and the freedom out of which he loves us. But are we ready to allow God the freedom to have some desires of his own? Are we ready to admit that he may be gladdened when his offer of love is discovered and hurt when that offer is frustrated or rejected? I do not think that such feelings would reflect a divine inadequacy. In fact, they may even account for why human beings experience the same feelings, since we are fashioned in God's image. Our own feelings of gladness and hurt are rooted in the acceptance or rejection by others of our freely offered love. Perhaps through such feelings we participate, however dimly, in God's experience of satisfaction and disappointment.

To look upon God as having feelings about us is probably

not the way in which we have been taught to *think* about God,
but it is close to the way in which we have been taught to *relate* to
God. Our thinking about God generally centered on his knowing all things and his ability to do all things, but our experience
tended to bypass these attributes as we imagined God to be
pleased, or angry, or disappointed, or caring, or lonely. How
much of that experience is to be trusted?

God draws us to ever greater freedom, but freedom is
diminished by fear. If God is someone we are afraid of, then we
cannot be truly free as his sons and daughters. I recall a man
whose boy had fallen very ill had convinced himself that God
was punishing him through his son's sickness. We want to ask
about the kind of God that man has been praying to for so long.
He was a God who stirs up fears and who never had a son in
whom he could delight. Has God been punishing Adam all these
years through misfortunes inflicted upon his offspring? If God
created the world out of love, and if he is indeed changeless,
then how could his feeling toward the world be different now
than it was in the beginning?

Again, there are some Christians who are afraid to offer
themselves to God. They have been told about God's love, but
when in prayer God invites them to make a complete gift of
themselves to him, they flinch. If they tell God that they are
placing themselves totally in his hands, it occurs to them that he
may accept the offering. And they do not know what he might
do next. He might ask them to give up a loved one, or lose their
good health, or suffer an economic or social reversal.

It takes years for us to appreciate the Christian doctrine of
creation. There is no difficulty in affirming that God made the
world, since the world had to have a beginning. While we know
that God made the world, we frequently do not comprehend
why.

Taking Scripture at Its Word

The language of the Bible abounds with metaphor, but
metaphorical language is not untruthful. When Scripture reports how God feels about his people, when a prophet like

Jeremiah experienced rejection, loneliness, desertion, and being misunderstood, or when Jesus experienced the same range of prophetic feelings, what prevents us from regarding these experiences as something God also feels through his prophet or through his Son?

The Lord has extended himself to us and has chosen to share our life in order that we might come to share in his. If we maintain that love, peace, freedom, and joy are experiences which signal the active presence of God's Spirit, then what about disappointment, loneliness, and hurt? If we can share sometimes in the satisfaction God enjoys because of us, then why not also an opportunity to participate in his feeling when great love is rejected? Indeed, to experience these things is a grace which St. Ignatius Loyola begged for in the part of his *Spiritual Exercises* devoted to the suffering and death of Christ:

> The third prelude is to ask for what I desire. Here it will be to ask for sorrow, compassion, and shame because the Lord is going to His suffering for my sins. . . . In the Passion it is proper to ask for sorrow with Christ in sorrow, anguish with Christ in anguish, tears and deep grief because of the great affliction Christ endures for me. . . . I will make an effort to be sad and grieve because of the great sorrow and suffering of Christ our Lord. . . . I will rouse myself to sorrow, suffering, and anguish by frequently calling to mind the labors, fatigue, and suffering which Christ our Lord endured.

This seems clearly to be an invitation to enter into the divine experience at least in some way. Should we not therefore take Scripture seriously? When the Father says, "You are my Son, whom I love; with you I am well-pleased" (Mk. 1:11), are we not to believe that God is delighted? Or when Jesus teaches us to trust God and out of that trust to ask for anything in his name, are we not to believe that God favors the prayer of those who remain faithful to his Son? Or when the Lord Jesus says to Paul, "Why do you persecute me?" (Acts 9:4), why should we not believe that even the glorified Lord feels the pain inflicted upon his brothers and sisters?

I realize, of course, that Scripture also attributes some barbaric acts to God, and the reader may wonder what keeps us from admitting the validity of those reports as well. Did God order up the slaughter of infants as we read, for example, in the Book of Joshua? Did God intend to grant the prayers for bloody revenge that we often find in the psalms?

Well, we would not be the first Christians to voice such misgivings about the Old Testament and a complete answer would require many pages. But we should not let the objection obscure what we do know. The fact is that we can discriminate between those things about God which ennoble us, reaffirm us, and lead us to deeper freedom, and those things which reduce our stature, which cause us to repent the torment inflicted by religious people who enlisted God on the side of their narrow schemes, and which prevent us from understanding the Jesus who cried, "Father, forgive them, for they do not know what they are doing" (Lk. 23:34).

Called To Imitate the Divine Freedom

From what we have said so far, it might appear that we are trying to tailor God in terms of human feelings. We experience rejection, God experiences rejection, and so we are able to understand God better. We become angry, God becomes angry, and so human anger is somehow vindicated; it is all right to be angry. But this conclusion would be a mistake. The point of our discussion is not so much to focus upon God's experience in order to understand ourselves better or to confer respectability upon our feelings. That may happen. But the point is to contemplate the Lord's experience in order to share more intimately in his life. And this brings us to the greatest Christian challenge.

As the Church Fathers noted long ago, and as the Gospel writers themselves perceived, Christ is the key which unlocks the meaning of Scripture. Whenever a Christian in reading the Old Testament senses some resistance to a God portrayed differently from the God we are familiar with in Christ, then we have a warrant, in keeping with our tradition, for putting that portrayal aside.

Above all else, Christ reveals God to be free. God freely created the world as a prelude to freely communicating himself to creatures made in his image. Because he is free, God has nothing to lose. Since he is without pride or self-pity, he carries no grudges and strikes no revenge. Since he is free, his language is utterly truthful; he has nothing to hide. Because he is free, there is nothing God cannot let go of in order to win our love. Christ sacramentalizes what the mystery of God's freedom is all about.

The great freedom of God is simply another way of naming the selflessness of his love, and this divine character qualifies whatever feelings are ascribed to him. Human anger is as frequently laced with hurt pride and egoism as human love is touched by expectations of its being reciprocated. Selfless loving comes hard. Sacrifice is the proper word for it; the cross is its rightful sign.

Only a free person can turn the other cheek, walk the extra mile, and readily forgive insult and injury. Only a free person can become angry without succumbing to bitterness, and suffer without calling for vengeance. Only one who is free will show real compassion in the face of grotesque evil. Only a God who is freedom itself can look at the world's sin and intensify his desire to give his people new life. Is this not the God we find in Christ?

This accounts for why God alone can forgive sins. Forgiveness is built upon compassion and compassion rests on freedom. In his compassion God offers the world an unqualified acceptance, which is something no one else can do. We are worthwhile, he says, because we belong to him. Who besides God is so free that mercy should be his second name?

God's single intention in our behalf is to share his life. In total freedom, he is like the man who persists in knocking at his neighbor's door and finally rouses him from bed so that he might get him a few loaves of bread (Lk. 11:5–8), or he is like the widow who wears out the unjust judge (Lk. 18:1–5). God stays faithful to his offer of life no matter how many times we pass it by. His self-esteem does not suffer; he does not worry about his reputation; he clings to nothing.

The great challenge confronting believers is the invitation to share in the experience of God's own freedom. Through prayerful attention to the words and example of Christ, our experience will be stretched and purified as we struggle to share in the love and compassion with which God feels the world. We must carefully ponder the reason why God created the world, why he sustains it and carries it along, and why he can be so patient with its weakness.

I do not think it is too much to say that, having aimed at being in communion with us, God rejoices when that aim is being fulfilled. And when human selfishness frustrates his desire, God knows the sadness of an unrealized possibility.

Learning To Let God Be Free

One of the difficulties we face in becoming people of God is the disproportion between our freedom and the Lord's. As a result, the habit of not allowing God the full measure of his freedom can be a constant affliction.

Jesus spent much of his ministry correcting people's narrow understanding of God. God's love and mercy exceeded what even the prophets had expected. For example, the parable about the vineyard workers who receive the same wage though some labored long hours and others had worked only a few (Mt. 20:1–16) was calculated to force Jesus' audience to reflect. Something in the parable irritates us because it seems unfair. Is it right that those who work briefly for the kingdom should be rewarded as much as those who labor for a lifetime? Should the Gentiles receive as much of an inheritance as Israel? After all, the Jewish people had been waiting centuries for salvation. They had endured cruel bondage, wandered in deserts, endured the scoldings of the prophets and the destruction of their lands. What had the Gentiles suffered, and how long had they been waiting? And thus jealousy begins to rear its ugly head. "Or are you envious because I am generous?" (Mt. 20:15). The parable directly challenges us with the disproportion between our freedom and the Lord's.

Again, in urging his disciples to pray for their enemies, Jesus did not immediately add, "and God will eventually crush them for you." Authentic forgiveness is marked by the earnest prayer that God will show mercy even to one's enemies and that together with our enemies we may one day behold the face of God in his glory. Christ's own example dramatized how much he believed this teaching, an example which the Spirit will inspire his disciples to imitate:

> While they were stoning him, Stephen prayed, "Lord Jesus, receive my spirit." Then he fell on his knees and cried out, "Lord, do not hold this sin against them" (Acts 7:59).

The whole of Jesus' life reveals a beautiful interior freedom—the company he kept, the friendships he struck, the kinds of places he would frequent: the Lord does not fast, he is accused of being a friend of drunkards, he moves in the company of sinners and those who harvest the taxes, and he lets himself be anointed by a sinful woman in public. He enjoys banquets and visits hovels as well as rich estates.

Neither does Jesus try to win public esteem and support for his cause. He flees from those who would make him king when they realize what he can do with a few loaves of bread. He insisted upon repentance and called upon men and women to interiorize the command to perfection embodied in the Law: "Be perfect, therefore, as your heavenly Father is perfect" (Mt. 5:48). If the rich are told to share with the poor, the poor are enjoined to trust in God and to forgive their enemies.

Several years ago, the question of amnesty for draft evaders stirred a lot of controversy. I noticed that middle-aged couples who were working diligently to establish themselves socially and financially were more likely to be threatened by amnesty-talk than many elderly people whose lives were drawing to a close and who had greater reason to hope for divine amnesty than for the ongoing stability of the social establishment. If we knock out the props of reputation, career, and the other marks of earthly success, then what shall we fall back upon? Life will gradually loosen the props from under each one of us; in time we may appreciate the deeper meaning of Jesus' teaching on forgiveness. Isn't it easier to think of amnesty when we are seeking divine pardon for the sins of a lifetime than when we are asked daily to forgive one another?

Amnesty threatens people because it strikes at the system of reward and penalty upon which our law and society are based. But God is free, and he pardons absolutely. Our resistance to the notion of amnesty insinuates itself into our religious life and becomes a resistance to the Lord. He may appear too good, and we may find ourselves reluctant to allow him such freedom. "Or are you envious because I am generous?"

Challenged by the Humanness of Jesus

Just as Jesus challenged the people to re-examine their view of God, so too he challenges us with his own humanness. The Gospels are explicit about the humanity of Jesus: he sleeps (Mt. 8:24), he grows tired and thirsty (Jn. 4:6–7), he experiences deep emotion (Jn. 11:33), he prays (Mk. 1:35), he becomes angry with Peter (Mk. 8:33), with the Pharisees (Mt. 23:13ff), and with salesmen in the temple (Jn. 2:13–16). The Gospels present a Jesus who is tempted (Mk. 1:12–13), not sure of everything (Mk. 13:32), even afraid of his death (Mk. 14:35; Lk. 22:42; Mt. 26:39). Jesus is so ordinary—just a carpenter's boy from Nazareth—that his very ordinariness and familiarity become a source of scandal (Lk. 4:13–30).

A Jesus who is so human can be as threatening as a God who is too merciful. In fact, the connection between Jesus and God becomes complete when Jesus starts to forgive sins: "Who can forgive sins but God alone?" (Mk. 2:7) A God who comes so close to us is a God who must think that we are capable of greatness. But that greatness is not a piety of lengthy prayers, the asceticism of frequent fasting, the coins contributed to a church treasury, and the like. Instead, Jesus called for a greatness defined by forgiveness, compassion, service, and trust in God's love.

If Christians should find themselves offended by the humanness of Jesus, preferring instead a more exalted Lord to adore and follow, then it seems to me that they will miss a great truth of Christian faith. They will not share the experience of being a companion with Jesus, a Jesus who understands them because he has really shared the human condition. By living with Christ and in Christ, however, we can come to know and love God as Jesus experienced him. By living our life in union with Christ, we travel the same journey of faith that he did—dependent upon the Father, hopeful, and sure of his love.

Because of Christ, we believe that our journey to God will be achieved through our humanness and not despite it. In other words, the freedom which we allow to Jesus by accepting him in his humanness measures the freedom with which we accept our own humanity as the place where we must find God. Unless we learn to respect God's freedom to be truly human in Christ, we shall not leave God enough room to fashion us in the way he fashioned Jesus. For it has pleased God to make human beings holy by taking on their created nature. God has revealed to us in Jesus how his creative design, through a profound prayer of obedience on our part, can penetrate and transform human beings so as to establish their complete union with him.

Freedom Through Obedience

There is a connection between human freedom and the realization that we always belong to God. God calls us to deepen our liberty, not by becoming more autonomous, but by learning how to respond to his call. That means taking responsibility for our lives and imitating the example of Christ.

If we are careful to understand submission to the will of God in the active sense of freely cooperating with his designs for the world, then we can say that Christian freedom achieves its highest expression in obedience to God's will. Such obedience is sometimes risky, frightening, confusing, and even crucifying. It involves prayerful discernment and it demands distinguishing between complacency and resignation, between cooperation and control.

Obedience might well serve as another name for faith; it is a reverent listening to every word that comes from the mouth of God. People of faith discover that God's word is life-giving (Dt. 8:3). Following that word qualifies us to be members of the Lord's family: "My mother and brothers are those who hear God's word and put it into practice" (Lk. 8:21). The obedience of Jesus is also life-giving; it became the source of our salvation:

> Although he was a son, he learned obedience from
> what he suffered, and once made perfect, he became
> the source of eternal salvation for all who obey him
> (Heb. 5:8–9).

Christians learn the true nature of obedience by contemplating and living out what they observe in Jesus. In his company we learn from him what it means to be a person of faith and how to listen to God's word; we are taught to follow that word wherever it beckons us. But this is the way of freedom, and Jesus knew it. And so, on the night before he died, Jesus prayed to God, "Father, I want those you have given me to be with me where I am" (Jn. 17:24). And when those first two disciples were following Jesus by the bank of the Jordan, Jesus turned to ask them, "What do you want?" They replied, "Rabbi, where are you staying?" And he said, "Come, and you will see" (Jn. 1:37–39). The experience of being one of Jesus' disciples could be summed up as learning how to live where Jesus is; for where Jesus is, there lies our freedom.

Obstacles Along the Way

For Jesus, there was only one way to lead his life, and that was the way of his Father. For us, there is also but one way, and that way is Christ's. Our freedom and our peace depend upon our being with Christ on *his* way, however, and not along some way of our own that we ask Jesus to join from time to time.

Problems arise as we substitute our own way for the Lord's; we may be comforted by the fact that the apostles experienced those problems too.

"You ask with the wrong motives" (Jas. 4:3). The Gospels teach that the way of Christ is the way of obedience. Christ's obedience was the response of a son to his father, and that response only makes sense to us, considering the fate of Jesus, in view of his profound trust in the Father's love and wisdom. All Christian obedience is patterned on that of Jesus. It calls for a mature freedom which has been seasoned by prayer; it discovers and respects God's will for the world. Such obedience cannot be understood apart from the dying and rising of Christ, since in those events we see how our God is on the side of life. He will not allow death to steal anyone who obeys his words and cooperates with his plan for the human race.

Many devout people feel quite at home with language about accepting the will of God. When they ask God for something and events transpire as they had hoped, then they feel (and perhaps rightly so) that God heard their prayer. If they fail to receive what they asked for, then they can relax in the conviction that God did not want them to have it. In either case, God will not lose.

The difficulty with this approach to prayer is that one never has to wrestle with the mystery of God; one need only plead with him more earnestly or accept his will more patiently. Many members of the people of God do not escape so easily.

Often in our prayer we ask God for favors like success at a job, financial security, improved health, a rich harvest, and so on. Our needs are endless, and most of them are innocent and good. And since what we are requesting is objectively good and reasonable, why would the Lord not grant them? Sometimes, however, we are not granted these things. Sometimes we find ourselves identifying with the experience of Job.

None of us would doubt that the world belongs to God. He alone can judge what is finally worthwhile, good, and successful. Jesus warned his disciples not to judge others, but is it likely that he meant we should never take a stand on the goodness or evil in a person's actions? Jesus made such judgments when he excoriated the Pharisees, and Paul passed judgment about immorality in Corinth, and the modern Church has made a judgment about the immorality of the arms race. Such judgments have to be made.

Perhaps Jesus had something different in mind. Whereas we tend to size someone up in terms of what we can observe in his or her behavior, God sees the struggle of heart and will. He observes the testing of soul and purification of spirit. Christ's warning, therefore, reminds us that we have no way of observing another person's interior combat. The danger of passing judgment on others is that we impose our standard of a successful and upright life instead of the Lord's.

In the same way, when we come to ask God for what seems to us reasonable and good, our faith should remind us that God finally must be the judge of what is truly reasonable. National defense seems to be a good and reasonable aim, but does that mean that God can be invoked to bless the weapons of war and those who build them?

There should be no doubt about the Lord's concern for us; he remains steadfast in his goodness. But precisely because he is so concerned, he is likely to be discriminating about those things which will further or impede our well-being and the salvation of the entire human family. What would be God's stake in the manufacture of junk foods? Can he be coopted by a prayer service into blessing a nuclear arsenal? Does he have a vested interest in electric can-openers or hair-dryers? This may sound silly, but nevertheless we ought to examine the assumptions behind our style of living. It is a very real possibility that God has little interest in the gadgets, kinds of food, style of clothes, and so on, which we take for granted as part of life.

It is possible that much of our business, our way of life, our social and educational values, our economic goals, our military needs, and even some church activities have little or nothing to do with God's overall aim for the world. We may be asking him for his blessing without realizing that our aims and God's oppose each other.

This indeed is food for thought. When I was in grammar school, our class prayed one day for good weather at the class picnic, and I started to wonder if some nearby farmer were begging the Lord for rain on his tomatoes. Ever since, I have to confess to some chagrin when I want to ask the Lord for good weather. "Who of you by worrying can add a single hour to his life?" Jesus told his disciples. "Since you cannot do this very little thing, why do you worry about the rest?" (Lk. 12:25–26). Now the picture is somewhat different, but the point remains true. How do we know for sure that our concerns are actually in our own best interest, or in the best interest of the whole people of God?

Maybe in our daily assessment of what is necessary and important, we do not leave God enough space to enter a disclaimer. The fact that things turn out as we had hoped does not prove that God heard our prayer. And the fact that we have not received what we wanted does not imply that the Lord was not listening. Recall the story of Queen Esther, who prayed that she would be strong enough to face a bold and fearsome king with courage in order to intercede with him on behalf of her people. When she finished her prayer and went to face the king, she fainted. Moved with pity, the king caught her in his arms and his heart changed as he held her (Book of Esther, chapters 14–15). Was her prayer answered in the way she expected?

Stumbling over the Law

Our attitude toward law can also be an obstacle to a ready respect of God's freedom. In the matter of legal observance, both Paul and Jesus experienced much opposition. The early Christians answered the charge of the scribes and Pharisees that Jesus did not obey Jewish religious law by asserting that Jesus himself was the New Law.

For the early Church, Christ was not a dead letter about legal prescriptions but the living law which had been revealed to his followers as their way, their truth, and their life. Jesus confronted the legal authorities with his example of healing, plucking grain, or forgiving sins on the Sabbath. He claimed that God's law was intended to be life-giving, not crippling, and so he healed paralytics on the Sabbath. Paul argued that faith in

Christ was indeed more life-giving and justifying than the law of Moses; one need not be Jewish in order to be Christian.

Let us reflect on the issue for a moment.

By ordinary human standards, a person's integrity is often measured in terms of how well he or she obeys the law. To be law-abiding is a highly regarded civic virtue. Yet fidelity to a legal code, even to the civil laws of the land, becomes a menace unless the Spirit inhabits our religious life. Without the Spirit, the criterion of virtue simply reduces to not-breaking the law. Violators upset the stability of our social system and are prosecuted; serious offenders are sent to prison.

But God operates no jails. He does not judge us on the basis of how many times we broke his law, but on the basis of how many times we attempted earnest repentance. God's law is a summons to holiness. It never merely sets the ideal of what Christians ought to do. An ideal only indicates the abstract standard by which behavior is judged. Instead, the law of God both lures and invites us further along the path of holiness. In this sense, Jesus does indeed become the new law: not as an abstract ideal of perfection but as the one who personally calls us to renewal and holiness. God's law breathes; its breath is the Spirit of life.

How we look upon the purpose of law may figure into how we find the Lord. What does God truly expect of us? How should we judge ourselves or other people? It is salutary to reflect occasionally on why the Jewish leaders had so subverted the meaning of the Law that they could insist before Pilate, "We have a law, and according to that law he must die, because he claimed to be the Son of God" (Jn. 19:7). They were threatened by genuine freedom. Jesus was too free.

Respecting the Freedom of Our Neighbor

A final obstacle to our becoming fully people of God is our reluctance to allow our friends and neighbors to be free. Just as we can hedge the Lord by reducing him to expectations tailored to suit our smallness instead of letting him enlarge our thoughts and desires, so we can let our fears contain the personal growth of those closest to us. In either case, the mystery of God is diminished.

It is not easy to live with differences between ourselves and those around us. Whether it is a matter of hair style, types of clothing, taste in food and movies, or views on politics and religion, differences are hard to tolerate. We tend to associate with those who think the way we do, who share the same interests, who aspire to the same lifestyle, and who perhaps attend the same church. Often we put up with strangers and neighbors better than with our own families because different ideas and personalities are less threatening to us when we do not have to live with them. The closer we come to one another, the more we are called upon to respect another person's freedom.

It is always a danger, though, that human beings want so strongly to be secure and unthreatened that they tend to suppress differences close to home by the demands they make on their families and friends. We resort to subtle means of reward and punishment in order to bend others into conformity. How often do people offer or withdraw signs of affection in order to fashion a child or a spouse or a friend into their own image and likeness?

So much of human life throughout history has been wasted in political and religious persecution for no other reason than that men and women could not stand to live with differences. How many families have been driven apart by venomous words because husbands and wives, fathers and daughters, mothers and sons were attempting to fashion one another into their own likeness? I do not mean that we should ignore one another's mistakes, but I do mean that we cannot thwart one another's freedom without hurting ourselves. Let me give an example.

A teenager was describing his family life. Nothing he did apparently pleased his father, and the father let him know it. His grades were never high enough, his manners never refined enough, his clothes never clean enough, his friends never mature enough. The father was short on praise and high on complaint. The most common phrases went like this: "You can't do anything right. . . . Do it the way I told you or don't do it at all. . . . If I've told you once, I've told you a thousand times. . . ."

The boy was not a genius, and probably was no angel either. But he was a fine child, his tears were honest, and his story sounded so familiar. The father, it occurred to me, did not need a son; he needed a mirror. Many children, many husbands and wives, and many a friend knows the pain of this sort of experience.

People have been created to mirror God, not one another. God does not look forward to our reflecting back a truncated vision of himself, nor does he appreciate our distorting his image in one another. That is why he gave us Christ to look at.

A Lesson from the Old Testament

If we believe the prophets, God was not all that eager to leave his mobile dwelling and settle into the temple, even though someone of the stature of Solomon had built it. Once religious life becomes established so that men and women can point and exclaim, "There is God; he belongs to us," religion is stifled. The living God cannot be contained by a temple or a tabernacle; in fact, his saving activity cannot be confined to one single religious community. Grace belongs to God. The providence and transcendence of God will not be measured by our ideas of him.

One feature of the Exodus and the wandering in the desert is God's freedom of movement which was symbolized by the ark of the covenant and the pillar of fire. Perhaps he was instructing the tribes of Israel about his freedom and theirs. As long as God remains free, his people stay free. In domesticating the Lord, in laying exclusive ownership to his presence and Spirit, the people suffer. They shorten their own freedom and abridge the possibility of experiencing real peace.

In the same way, by seeking to control or manipulate one another, we not only violate another's freedom; we also surrender our own. By laying down the terms under which other people are to relate to us, we give in to our fears of being rejected. But the drive to security which might tempt us to bend another into our likeness usually results in the bitterness of further insecurity and fear.

The Heavens Proclaim the Glory of God

Often in the late autumn and winter, but also on some cool summer nights, if you are lucky to find a place where the sky is free of haze and reflected city light, you will discover the stars. There is a freshness about finding them when you haven't seen them for a while. They sky is charged to pull human eyes heavenward. If you haven't seen the stars for some time, then the night sky takes on a certain strangeness. For without the sun we no longer see the earth's boundaries of cloud and sea; there are only the silent reaches of starred darkness. The earth is set into perspective against the measureless space reserved for the heavenly bodies. The wonder of it is refreshing; the stars call you out of yourself.

Meditating on the freedom of God also calls us out of ourselves. It illumines us about the God who surpasses whatever our minds and hearts imagine about him. Every little stretching of our knowledge about God both humbles us and pulls us further along as we become people of God. God is free. Out of his freedom he created the world and summoned us to life. What response are we to make to the love of God? If from time to time we forget the essential truth about ourselves and behave as if the world belonged to us and we were the creators, then at least we have the stars to remind us whose glory the heavens proclaim.

5   Looking for God
in the Right Places

No one can really "prove" the existence of God to a non-believer. The world in which we live is going to look the same whether we believe in God or not. But our world is like a book that needs to be read and interpreted, and people of faith realize that the book of life cannot be satisfactorily interpreted apart from God. Any attempt to demonstrate God's existence will not make God appear, like a rabbit from a magician's hat; the demonstration will not tell us anything we did not already know.

People must be led to see that neither they nor their world makes any sense, ultimately, unless God exists. And if he exists, God is already in the world. By paying close attention to our experiences, by listening to the desires of our own heart, and by openness to the many voices of those who have found God, we gradually learn to read the world correctly. The world has a lot to tell us about who and what we are.

Christians tend to discover Christ in some very unlikely places. St. Luke recounts an episode when Paul and Silas, having delivered a slave girl of a demon, were unjustly accused of inciting trouble:

The crowd joined in the attack against Paul and Silas, and the magistrates ordered them to be stripped and beaten. After they had been severely flogged, they were thrown into prison, and the jailer was commanded to guard them carefully. Upon receiving such orders, he

put them in the inner cell and fastened their feet in the
stocks.
     About midnight Paul and Silas were praying and
singing hymns to God, and the other prisoners were
listening to them (Acts 16:22-25).

The scene is characteristically Christian. Paul and Silas have
been unjustly arrested, beaten, jailed, and fastened, and yet we
find them in the middle of the night singing and praising God.
With some justification they could be called the maddest of
men, unless, of course, in that situation they had somehow
found God to be present. Even a prayer for speedy deliverance
would have made more sense, or perhaps a prophetic complaint
or lament would have been a more intelligible response to their
treatment. But singing hymns to God? How did God's presence
to them in that cell, about midnight, evoke not feelings of self-
pity and lamenting, but of prayer and song?
     Luke reported a similar incident in one of the earlier chap-
ters of the Acts of the Apostles. Peter and the other apostles had
been arrested and beaten for preaching about Jesus, and Luke
wrote:

The apostles left the Sanhedrin, rejoicing because they
had been found worthy of suffering disgrace for the
Name. Day after day, in the temple courts and from
house to house, they never stopped teaching and pro-
claiming the good news that Jesus is the Christ (Acts
5:41–42).

How do we account for this sort of reaction—a reaction
mirrored in the lives of Christian saints down through the
centuries?

The Spirit's Imprint

     In his book *Jesus and the Spirit*, the contemporary British
Scripture scholar James Dunn argued that we can gauge what
the word "Spirit" means in the New Testament by looking at

what the early Christians perceived the Spirit to be doing among them. What was the Spirit doing? The Spirit was tracing God's family likeness upon believers. That likeness took its measure from the person of Christ, particularly in the event of his dying and rising.

Through his death and resurrection Christ had revealed the mystery of how deeply God wanted to affirm life. God created us in order to share life, and in raising Jesus from the grave, the Son in whom he was well pleased (Mt. 17:5), God was telling us that he will not allow what he loves to perish—neither in the case of Jesus, his Son, nor in the case of his Son's disciples. In the resurrection God said "Yes" to the life Jesus had led; in the divine plan, life and not death must exert the final claim on human existence. The Father will raise us too, provided that when he looks upon us he finds there the family likeness. That is to say, if we are to join Christ in his glory we must first follow him in his suffering. In becoming more and more conformed to his image, we make the same offering of our lives to God which Jesus made.

The family likeness is the sign of the cross. It is the sign which begins and ends Christian life, the sign with which we mark ourselves at the beginning and conclusion of every prayer. The sign of the cross becomes our great act of faith by which we say to God, "Let the sign of your Son's life be traced across mine, that you might see and love in me the same things you see and love in Christ."

Wherever then Christians found themselves having to endure patiently either the daily cares of human life or the humiliation and persecution brought on by their witnessing to the Gospel, they learned to read their experience in terms of the experience of Christ. They began to experience in themselves his dying and rising. Though burdened or beaten, they felt, oddly enough, joyous, since what had happened to Jesus was now happening to them. The Christ whom they had encountered in faith drew them to taste the power of God that worked through human weakness.

The limiting case in which God's power worked, the situation wherein men and women are at their weakest, was death itself. But just as Christians were discovering new joy and power in the routine of life, so they were tasting a new confidence and freedom in the face of death. As far as Paul was concerned, the Spirit's presence could be tested by the way Christians were being fashioned, both in their living and in their dying, into the image of Christ. The test consisted of how clearly their lives had been signed with the Lord's cross.

The Example of Paul

One especially difficult episode in Paul's life involved the Corinthian church where his very apostleship had been seriously challenged. Paul rested his defense, not on his vision of the risen Christ, nor on his charismatic gifts. Instead, as we read in the later chapters of the Second Letter to the Corinthians, Paul appealed to his apostolic experience wherein he had come to know companionship with the suffering and weak Christ:

> Therefore, I will boast all the more gladly about my
> weaknesses, so that Christ's power may rest on me.
> That is why, for Christ's sake, I delight in weaknesses,
> in insults, in hardships, in persecutions, in difficulties.
> For when I am weak, then I am strong (2 Cor. 12:9–10).

In the persecution, the betrayals, the beatings, the hunger and shipwreck, the nakedness and thirst and anguish over the infant churches, Paul saw that his life was being patterned after the life of Jesus.

Why did he welcome such things? What could possibly induce anyone in his right mind to *desire* hardships like these? Only an intense longing to be a companion of Christ, a love that wants to be wherever Jesus is, explains Paul. He wanted to experience God through experiencing the life of his Son. In this experience Paul knew the real nature of Christ's resurrection:

> I want to know Christ and the power of his resurrection
> and the fellowship of sharing in his sufferings, becom-

ing like him in his death, and so, somehow, to attain to
the resurrection from the dead (Phil. 3:10–11).

To use James Dunn's words, Jesus is the charisma of God.
Each believer's life is charismatic to the extent that we are being
formed anew through the mystery of Jesus' dying and rising.
Each believer becomes a new creation as his or her life is
informed by the sign of the cross. It is not the working of
miracles or the uttering of prophecies, not fancy sermons or
speaking in tongues; it is the sign of the cross, gradually being
etched across one's life, which marks the presence and action of
the Spirit of Jesus.[1]

As we saw in the first chapter, only God (because he is the
Creator) can determine whether or not his creation turned out
successfully; it is his designs which must be accomplished. Christian faith understands that Christ alone is the standard of success when it comes to human living. He is the norm for what
human beings will become if they are prepared to let God keep
his work of creation going on in them. When Paul exhorts his
churches to put on Christ, he is intimating that unless they do
so, God will not "see" them. For the Father has eyes only for his
Son; when he looks out over the world, it is Christ that he
notices. Thus we must clothe ourselves in his image (Gal. 3:27),
becoming a new creation (Eph. 4:24), so that God might spot us
too when he looks over his world. Being a Christian is a matter
of taking on the family likeness; Paul knew that that likeness was
the sign of the cross.

The Sign of the Cross on Today's Believers

Is the event of becoming a new creation more difficult to
penetrate today? Was it simpler for Paul to comprehend than for
us?

We live in a streamlined, efficiency-oriented culture which
finds disorder hard to bear. Sickness and pain, to be sure, have
not been regarded as good things in themselves in any age, but
today they are more likely to be regarded as unnatural. Illness is

an inconvenience, especially for those who do not happen to be sickly.

All of us have encountered irate motorists who fume over a red light or a car which has stalled in traffic. We have probably seen someone grow out of temper because of a busy-signal on the telephone. As people become increasingly impatient, indifferent, or upset with the wider human concerns around them, they resent being inconvenienced by the breakdowns, the unreliability, and the misfortunes of our times.

Yet, is it not possible that all the instrusions upon the ordinary and predictable course of daily life disclose in some manner the silent presence of a God who invites us to a deeper peace? The very things we run away from may turn out to be instrumental in putting us in touch with the alienation from ourselves that we feel. Sooner or later, we need to face up to our unwillingness to be interrupted and inconvenienced by some of the most natural and predictably human events.

Creaturehood need not always be a bothersome experience. God reaches out to us in the welcome experiences of ambling through a park, gazing at a night sky, watching the ocean tides, talking and laughing with our children and friends, listening to music, enjoying a dinner; the list is endless. But one's spiritual sense requires fine tuning in order to discern the Lord's presence in the experiences which make up our lives, whether they are unpleasant experiences that we cannot avoid or the happy ones we leave little time for. If life is not to be burdensome, we must put aside time for quiet thought and for speaking with friends who are also looking for the Lord as they make the journey of faith.

The Inevitability of Diminishment

It would probably sound overly pious to say that life provides us with many occasions to suffer, so instead of talking about suffering (and the risk of coming down with a martyr complex) let us adopt Teilhard de Chardin's term "diminishment" from *The Divine Milieu*. The reality will be the same, but diminishment further connotes the slow process of learning to let go. Diminishment is the hard side of being a creature; it is not something we choose so much as something which happens to us. The labor of making a living and supporting a family, the drudgery of sleepless nights with young children, the worry and heartache over what happens to friends and loved ones, maybe an accident or an unwanted divorce: the list winds on. It is the tale of life's diminishments. If we add to this list the feelings of inadequacy occasioned by the misfortune and poverty which make up the daily news, then our wills and tempers are worn even further.

But the heaviest burden we carry may not be our jobs, family demands, or the troubles of society. Our heaviest load might well be the impatient, inconstant, troubled, quick-to-judge, selfish soul that each of us is. Among the burdens which Paul urged his readers to carry (Gal. 6:2) must be included the sinful self that each of us can lay claim to. I have to live with myself, but others have to live with me too. Thus we stand in need of one another's forgiveness and patience; both forgiveness and patience are forms of letting go.

The Diminishment of Religion

There is another sort of diminishment which we face because we are believers at a time when many people are either indifferent or openly hostile to religion. We have to bear the gnawing suspicion that faith no longer has anything to contribute to the world. People of God have to stand strong or else be swamped by nuclear buildup, famine, crime, racism, and sensuality—problems which can erode one's faith. Christians are going to become an increasingly tired people whose voice is less respected, whose values make little sense, and whose example is watched for the least sign of hypocrisy. We may grow weary of the pervasive resistance to holiness and truth which has infected modern secular society, and which has gained entry into our own homes and perhaps into our very souls.

Family life has been affected. For we try to instruct our children about the Gospel, yet they do not listen. And if they listen, they often fail to understand; and if they claim to understand, they tell us the message is out of date. They appear not to see the real meaning of the message, insist that they do not see the message evidenced by our lives, our words fail to make the message clearer, and we are frequently at a loss to explain what and why we believe.

Religion used to seem so central a part of the week. At least people attended church, their lives felt secure, and their values and obligations were clearly spelled out. But even if we could return to those calmer days, we would probably find them empty and strange now, like an old toy discovered in the attic. If we examine our lives, each of us can locate that one thing we always wanted more than anything else and eventually, once we got it, put aside without regret. Many objects lie around us as reminders of how easily we lose interest in things that once seemed so precious. I suspect old religion is like that too.

In other words, Christians today experience a many-sided powerlessness. Indeed, this diminishment may not sound so dramatic as Paul's shipwreck and flogging, but it is real and painful nonetheless. "Who is weak, and I do not feel weak?" Paul asks. "Who is led into sin, and I do not inwardly burn?" (2 Cor. 11:29). With the apostle we must have recourse to the story of Christ in order to interpret our experience. The Lord endured diminishment, but at his weakest moment, at the hour of his death, God disclosed the deepest mystery. The world still belongs to God, and when creatures surrender to his designs for the world with trust and love, then God will unveil how mighty is the energy which draws the spirit to life. Out of the belly of death comes life; in weakness there can be great power. Paul discovered this truth when he met Christ.

Remembering Our Roots

As the Gospel speaks about taking up our cross daily, other religions teach about the necessity of suffering too. But Christian faith is distinct in its conviction that really there is but one cross, and it is Christ's. The motive power behind Christian faith impels us to desire to be where Christ is. That was Paul's prayer—to be with Christ, to share his fortune, to endure the same things, and to win the same prize. When the weakness of the people of God is illumined by the weakness of Christ, a fresh energy is discovered within our experience; that is the power of the Spirit.

Beyond the anxiety and discouragement of our lives and in our age there lies the deeper claim upon us to have hope. Indeed, we have not been made for ourselves but for God. His power works upon us, pressing against our weakness with the divine claim upon our faith. In the Gospel of John, Jesus tells the Jews that they are unable to recognize him as the One whom the Father has sent because they do not know where he came from. Ultimately, Jesus had come from God. But the point could be turned around: the reason why the Jews failed to recognize Jesus was that they had forgotten where *they* came from. They had lost touch with their roots and thus were incapable of recognizing God's goodness and life when they met it.

The stumbling block to faith, it seems to me, is not the presence of evil in the world but the presence of goodness. Evil is natural enough. When people lose sight of their own roots— our distant ancestor was Adam, who came from God (Lk. 3:38)—then they are likely to consider discouragement and greed, sadness and infidelity, as normal. But as people of faith we have the advantage of knowing that we have been made for great things. Men and women tend to stumble over their native goodness, especially when they find themselves hounded by a love that believes in their goodness. It is surprising and sometimes frightening to discover what happens to us when we are loved. How does one account for the fact that we are moved by what is good and animated by another's confidence in us?

Human beings differ much in terms of size and shape, color and language, gesture and talent, learning and handicap, virtue and vice. But beneath all these things, and central to being human, is the desire for life. To love and to be loved, to hope that our existence will prove worthwhile and that our struggles will not be in vain, and to pray that what is beautiful and good about those whom we love should not be devoured by the grave—this is what it means to be people of God; it is to trust these life-giving desires. The courage of such people to hope and not to capitulate to discouragement shows itself stronger than the irreverence and disaffection of unbelievers. God's weak ones demonstrate the greater strength because they dare to hope; and this is the problem of goodness.

And so we have turned to our roots as people of God. We discussed in the second chapter the basic desire for life, which is rooted in the Spirit. Trusting that this desire is not blind prepares the path for faith, and permitting that desire to guide our living paves the journey with hope. The sign of the cross is a Christian's great prayer of hope in the meaning and value of life. People who dare to hope and who live by faith reveal the imprint of the Christ-sign. In them the living God continues to draw the image of his Son; upon them the Spirit traces the sign of the cross.

Power Made Perfect Through Weakness

Powerlessness can be experienced in limitless ways, but each experience can be both unsettling and salutary. It is unsettling because it confronts us with the basic truth that we are not masters of the world, of our lives, of our routines, or of our neighbors. It will be salutary provided we are willing to admit that fact and not allow our resistance to creaturehood to harden. Life is hedged with all sorts of limitations. In attempting to deal with them, which is part and parcel of human life, we should not be deaf to the lesson which limitations can teach us about ourselves.

One summer I was spending some time in a remote village of northern India. The season was hot and steamy, the people were poor, and many children were sick. As the days went by, I grew aware of feelings of deep anger and resentment. I was unable to localize the feelings around any particular thing which had distressed me. At night, under the mosquito net, one could hear the muffled crunching of beetles chewing their way through the wooden beams which supported the thatched shelter. During the day we watched heavy clouds which promised rain pass right over us, leaving the village's rice plants to wither and die. Some people would starve, and they seemed to know it. One child sat on the ground while hordes of flies crawled through her eyes, nose, and mouth.

I guess that I had become angry at everything: at the people who had to live this way because they did not fight back, at the missions for not doing enough, at the corrupt local government that remained so insensitive to basic human needs, at human beings in general because of their greed, and at God for having made such a miserable world. The steady encroachment on human life and order became intolerable.

Among my belongings was a small silver cross which I treasured. I carried it in my shirt pocket, and during those days it symbolized a connection with the stable world back home. I was determined that it would survive the summer. One morning, as I stooped to enter the outhouse (its mud walls were caving outward and threatened imminent catastrophe for some poor soul), the cross fell from my pocket and into the hole. It sank into oblivion.

My anger far exceeded the value of the silver cross, but that was the last straw. I would have left the place immediately, except that we were far away from the train station; and the jeep, which had broken down six times on the trip from the station to the village, made the train seem six times as distant. At the time, the humor of it all escaped me.

All of us have had experiences similar to this one. Indeed, they are not the same outwardly, but they share the same inner experience. That morning it was not God that I was really angry with, nor with myself for having traveled to India, but with the whole damned world which functioned so inefficiently, so uncaringly, so consistently corrosive of human planning and effort. Even the Gospel passage which I later tried to read sounded out of place in that village; Christ did not seem to belong there. This was the passage, and it relates one of the early episodes in the career of the disciples:

One day as Jesus was standing by the Lake of Gennesaret (that is, the Sea of Galilee), with the people crowding around him and listening to the word of God, he saw at the water's edge two boats, left there by the fishermen, who were washing their nets. He got into one of the boats, the one belonging to Simon, and asked him to put out a little from the shore. Then he sat down and taught the people from the boat.

When he had finished speaking, he said to Simon, "Put out into deep water, and let down the nets for a catch."

Simon answered, "Master, we've worked hard all night and haven't caught anything. But because you say so, I will let down the nets."

When they had done so, they caught such a large number of fish that their nets began to break. So they signaled their partners in the other boat to come and help them, and they came and filled both boats so full they began to sink.

When Simon Peter saw this, he fell at Jesus' knees and said, "Go away from me, Lord; I am a sinful man!" For he and all his companions were astonished at the catch of fish they had taken, and so were James and John, the sons of Zebedee, Simon's partners.

Then Jesus said to Simon, "Don't be afraid; from now on you will catch men." So they pulled their nets up on shore, left everything and followed him (Lk. 5:1–11).

Notice that in this scene Peter declares his sinfulness even though he does not appear to have committed any sin. I was puzzled as to why Jesus' words and miracle elicited Peter's confession of sinfulness. Perhaps the reason was this.

The world Peter knew and had mastered was the Sea of Galilee. He had fished it, sailed it, weathered its seasons and storms. The lake was his livelihood, the situation he knew best, the place where he was in charge. It was the world he could predict and where he felt at home.

Jesus was the outsider, the teacher from Nazareth and a

carpenter's son. What could he possibly have known about fishing on Peter's lake? Perhaps what had begun to dawn on Peter that day was just how small his world was. Perhaps he realized how he, Peter, had such a grip on his world and was so thoroughly in charge of it, that he closed himself safely against God's new possibilities. Jesus entered Peter's life and tore that world open. When Luke adds at the end of the passage that they left everything to follow Jesus, he intends for us to ponder those words. "Left everything" meant that the companions took leave of the world they knew best. Matthew and Mark report that they simply "left their nets." And that was the heart of the matter. They left their nets, which meant the world they controlled, where they felt secure and at home, for a world that would no longer be their own but would belong to God.

This, it seems to me, is the same lesson that God would like each of us to learn also. Two worlds are available to us, one real and life-giving, free and secured by the surety of faith, a world where God is the Creator and we are his creatures. The other world is small, unreal in most respects, fastened in place by material possessions and the false values of men and women who are afraid of their creaturehood. It is a world that imprisons us in our own fears, and it compromises life by bartering truth for the sake of control. This is the world that is always fearful of the Russians, suspicious of the Chinese, and irritated by the Arabs. This is the world searching for new forms of entertainment, the good life, and fashionable things. It seeks comfort without discipline, companionship without commitment, and peace without justice. It is not a beautiful world in spite of its glamor; it is not the place where the mercifully close God wants his people to live.

And so it has been God's aim in Jesus to set us free from that world for his. Experiences of powerlessness in which the supports and cushions of one's world are shaken loose may not feel like God's grace. But if they rock us into the basic truth that creation belongs to God, that we belong to him, then they can be seen as signs of God's closeness as he draws us toward himself. This is the sort of experience the poet Gerard Manley

Hopkins had in mind in the opening lines of *The Wreck of the Deutschland*:

> Thou mastering me
> God! giver of breath and bread;
> World's strand, sway of the sea;
> Lord of living and dead;
> Thou hast bound bones and veins in me, fastened
> me flesh,
> And after it almost unmade, what with dread,
> Thy doing: and dost thou touch me afresh?
> Over again I feel thy finger and find thee.

Retrospect

My first reaction to the loss of that silver cross was not funny, and I imagine that Peter's reaction to Jesus' word to put down the nets which had been taken to shore for drying and mending must have shown some sign of exasperation. Did he not have a right to feel irritated when someone whom he did not yet know very well was directing him about fishing? In a moment of powerlessness it is natural to feel that God is a tease who bullies his creatures into submission, or that he intends to drag out of us a begrudging acknowledgement of our dependence upon him. When our world starts to become unstuck and we feel our creaturehood, how else could we react? Diminishment in any form involves suffering.

People of faith eventually understand that God is the only one who can teach us about who we are. As we contemplate Jesus, God shows that he neither pushes people around nor manipulates creation to tease his creatures. Instead, he attracts men and women to experience the freedom that comes from truth, and the peace that comes from intimate familiarity with himself. Jesus drew his disciples toward his vision of things by sharing his experience of the world, and out of their newly found freedom they risked (and finally surrendered) life itself.

This is the world that the Gospel likes to call the kingdom of God.

Each person's resistances to the Lord's action will be different. What we fear to lose or where we feel threatened will not be the same for everyone. And so, the fibers of the soul get parted differently. The heart of the problem does not consist in our possessing things or in our laboring to develop the riches of the earth. The problems arise when our attachments block the freedom and saving peace of God. Knowing the difference between honest concern for our welfare and the welfare of the world, and forgetful preoccupation with jobs, careers, and even with the basic needs of life, is the fruit of wisdom. Such wisdom comes from patiently learning the ways of God.

This education usually requires some experience of powerlessness and some wrestling with the Lord. The routine of everyday life reduces God to a casual and cozy presence. Until something out of the ordinary occurs, like losing a silver trinket or breaking your nets with too many fish, one may never learn how much the world belongs to God.

NOTE

1. James D. G. Dunn, *Jesus and the Spirit* (Philadelphia, 1975), pp. 318–338.

6 Faith and Reverence

The theme which has been running through these pages is creation. We have discussed God's stake in his handiwork, our response to his creative plan, and the gradual process by which we become genuinely people of God, and, therefore, people who reside in the truth. The last two chapters brought us to the matter of freedom—our freedom and the Lord's—and to the Spirit whose power imprints upon us the divine likeness, particularly through the experience of powerlessness. In this chapter we want to conclude our remarks by considering that as creatures we are called to a non-violent style of living which might simply be named reverence.

To link faith with reverence is, with Flannery O'Connor, to join mystery and manners. Because the earth belongs to God, the world is pervaded by mystery. But how much of that mystery we are able to perceive depends upon the courtesy we are prepared to show toward the things God has made. This is just to repeat what the psalmist declared:

> The earth is the Lord's, and everything in it,
> the world and all who live in it;
> for he founded it upon the seas
> and established it upon the waters (Ps. 24:1-2).

The earth is the neighborhood of God, and if we are to set foot into it, then our hearts should be schooled in the manners which God requires:

> Who may ascend the hill of the Lord?
> Who may stand in his holy place?
> He who has clean hands and a pure heart,
> who does not lift up his soul to an idol
> or swear by what is false (Ps. 24:3-4).

Pure hearts and clean hands belong to the manners which God favors. Only souls uncluttered by allegiance to the false gods made by human hands will experience the presence of God in creation.

The psalms provide numerous instances of how the well-mannered soul regards the earth with respect. So also do the many artists, poets, and musicians who draw our attention to the things which the Lord has made. Expounding on Psalm 100, St. Augustine wrote:

> For "his invisible things are clearly seen, being understood from what has been made." Look upon the things that are made, marvel at them, seek the author. If you are not like him, you will turn away; if you are like him, you will rejoice. And when, being like him, you have started to draw near and to perceive God distinctly, insofar as love grows in you, because God also is love, you will perceive a certain thing which you had been trying to say but could not express. For before you perceived God, you used to think that you could talk about him: you begin to perceive him, and then you realize that what you are experiencing cannot be expressed.

Once we have begun to experience God, Augustine tells us, we shall discover how hollow our talk about God has been. As we contemplate the world around us, noticing the presence of God in his works, good manners lead us to be quiet and to listen to the Lord in that stillness. "Be still, and know that I am God" (Ps. 46:10).

Reverence as the Form of Non-Violent Living

Part of the blame for why the world is losing some of the little faith that it has must lie, I think, with the modern world's mounting irreverence for the earth. The world is losing its manners. A responsive faith, which is more than knowledge about God and springs from a lively familiarity with him, will show itself in the way we regard and handle the things of this world. To the person of faith, the earth is the neighborhood of God, and reverence for the earth directs our step into mystery.

The Many Forms of Irreverence

There is nothing new about the irreverence inflicted upon people in the screaming and fighting which spill over from anger, nor about the violence suffered by language when words are twisted to hide the truth. There is the irreverence toward persons which appears in exploitation and cheating, and the disrespect done to our selves when the body is forced to distort the divine image which it harbors. Eyes are made to look at the obscene, ears are made to listen to gossip, tongues are bent into speaking slander, hands are stretched in clutching and hurting, stomachs swell with too much food, and minds grow out of shape from defending privilege and scheming ways to get ahead.

The energy crisis has forced us to take a second look at the environment, and it has caused us to explore measures for conservation. Yet these efforts will lack all due proportion unless they are serious about removing that massive irreverence toward the earth whereby its elements are pounded into bombs and other weapons. Nor should we forget how the earth is offended by the garbage that litters its cities and streets, by the spoiling of its oceans and air, by the tearing of the unborn from the womb. The earth is fouled when people are left to starve for want of food and love, and when slick campaigns persuade people to buy what they do not need and to need what they cannot afford. The problem is not that the world has lost faith and therefore has succumbed to irreverence. The problem is that, having lost its manners, the world is no longer able to apprehend mystery and truth.

The Non-Violent Life

However, there is a way of acting and thinking which is marked by piety and good manners. Such thinking is essentially non-violent and such living is naturally reverent. It knows, for example, when to be silent. It can listen to another person speak without planning a response while the other is yet talking. It can listen to God speak in the contemplative silence of prayer. For silence is non-violent. In silence one relaxes and notices the earth without lapsing into boredom. Out of silence we learn to recenter ourselves in terms of the world instead of recentering the world in terms of ourselves.

Noise, on the other hand, only serves to distract us from engaging the mystery around us; it drowns God's voice with televisions and billboards, gossip and daydreams, and the dozens of distractions which money can buy. Money is the enemy of manners as noise is the enemy of faith.

Non-violent thinking is not a work of intelligence but an attitude of life. Instead of trying to control life by figuring people out and making minute plans for the future, non-violent thinking welcomes the truth that the earth belongs to God. Instead of burping through life with the indigestion that comes with affluence or impatience, we learn to mind our manners, live simply, and treat the earth with respect. Most people, it seems to me, have not lost their innocence; they just have not discovered it. Innocence is simply the freshness with which we seize the mystery that is always unfolding around us. Thus the psalmist prayed:

> O Lord, our Lord,
>   how majestic is your name in all the earth!
> You have set your glory above the heavens.
>
> When I consider your heavens,
>   the work of your fingers,

the moon and the stars, which you have set in place,
what is man that you are mindful of him,
    the son of man that you care for him?
    (Ps. 8:1, 3-4).

The fate of religion is tied to reverence for the earth. The future of faith is tied to mundane things like trash on the roadside. Reverence for the earth disposes the heart for faith, and from faith there arise the great-souled responses of adoration, thanksgiving, and praise.

Courtesy requires something else. Respect for the earth will sound like twentieth-century romanticism unless it proceeds from an integral vision which finds the Spirit of God moving in and through all the members of the human family. Our vision may suffer from an occasional loss of integrity, and in that case God's own example provides a corrective. The resurrection of Jesus displays the full sweep of the gracious manners of our God.

Resurrection: God's Reverence for His Creation

No matter how clearly and smartly we think we have put together a statement about what human life is, we cannot adequately grasp the reality which we are. There is a mystery that embraces us. We are in no position to judge the value of our own life, or the life of another, or the value of human history.

Of course, we have a few clues as to what counts as important, which we uncover as we grow in our capacity to love others, and as we mature in our awareness of the world's sinfulness and its hunger for grace. Becoming a person of love is an achievement; it is holiness pure and simple. And, finally, it is the only work that matters. The achievement of lasting goodness, that is, what human beings contribute to the overall value of the universe by their struggles, joys, sufferings, and labors, transcends the perspective of any single generation. Since we have no insight into the core of another's soul—not even into our own—we cannot evaluate success or failure in the gradual sanctification of men and women. How human history enhances

creation, how it furthers God's aims for the universe, is something which good manners should prevent us from trying to
judge.

Creatures have never been in charge of producing the
lasting good of the world; they can only cooperate with its
production. This good obviously includes more than a civiliza-
tion's technical accomplishments. The world's basic worth consists, I believe, in what human beings become by what they do
and how they live. What happens in the case of any individual
existence runs deep into the heart of the world's mystery. It
concerns spirit and life which God alone can feel, appreciate,
and preserve. Only God can prevent what is truly an accomplish-
ment from being lost in a time-swept world.

Every achievement of the world's artists, builders, crafts-
men, inventors, explorers, musicians, thinkers, scientists, histo-
rians, and helpers makes up the aura surrounding the internal
development by which human beings become people of God.
Still, however much the light of the internal process of sanctification discharges into the world through so many cultural feats,
what finally happens within a human life is transparent only to
the eyes of God.

The Christian's confidence in the value of each person's
history stems from belief in the resurrection of Christ. In that
event, God issued his answer to the suffering and loss which
make up the painful side of the human story. It is life, not death,
that presses the final claim on us. In the resurrection God has
promised that he will not allow anything of value, the precious
stuff of human life, to perish from his sight. He will raise it to be
with himself. Resurrection pertains to the gracious manners of
our God.

The resurrection of Christ reveals the full dimensions of
God's creative design; it unveils the mystery behind every human life. God is courteous and kind. Reverence for his own self-
gift to creatures commits him to raising them from all the dying
which they endure. Through that gift, which we call grace,
creatures enrich the universe with their joyous appreciation of
the Lord's love, which surpasses all understanding. Resurrection is the ultimate kindness of a non-violent God.